Cross Talk

Preaching Redemption Here and Now

Sally A. Brown

Westminster John Knox Press
LOUISVILLE • LONDON

Book design by Drew Stevens
Cover design by Night & Day Design

First edition
Published by Westminster John Knox Press
Louisville, Kentucky

This book is printed on acid-free paper that meets the American National Standards Institute Z39.48 standard. ∞

PRINTED IN THE UNITED STATES OF AMERICA

08 09 10 11 12 13 14 15 16 17 — 10 9 8 7 6 5 4 3 2 1

Library of Congress Cataloging-in-Publication Data
Brown, Sally A. (Sally Ann)
  Cross talk : preaching redemption here and now / Sally A. Brown.—1st ed.
    p. cm.
  Includes index.
  ISBN 978-0-664-23002-9 (alk. paper)
  1. Jesus Christ—Crucifixion. 2. Holy Cross. 3. Preaching. I. Title.
BT450.B76 2008
232'.3—dc22   2007032147

This book is dedicated to my students, past and present. Their desire to preach the good news that God's promise is kept and being kept in Jesus Christ is the best reason I know for teaching or writing.

Contents

Acknowledgments

I am deeply grateful to my family, colleagues, and friends for their patience. All of them have endured my preoccupation with this work for far too long.

The friendship and insights of colleagues at Princeton Theological Seminary and elsewhere have sustained and inspired me at many crucial points. I am grateful to those who read the manuscript at various stages, particularly James F. Kay, whose suggestions have strengthened this work.

I am thankful, too, for the many pastors who have encouraged me to write this book and who, in a sense, sat alongside me in the study, keeping me focused on the real persons and real locations for which we preach. I hope they will recognize themselves in these pages.

I am grateful, as well, to my insightful editor at Westminster John Knox, Stephanie Egnotovich, who has supported this work, beginning to end; to my research assistants, Joshua McPaul, who gave such careful attention to the appendix; Kimberly A. Pepper and Susan Sytsma Bratt for their enthusiasm and assistance; and Rebecca Jordan Heys for her diligent help on the index; and to faculty secretaries Lois Haydu, Judith Attride, and Joan Blyth, whose skills have been invaluable.

Introduction

The subject of this book is one that theologians are discussing more and more, while preachers seem to speak of it less and less: the death of Jesus. In the last twenty years, the significance of the death of Jesus for Christian faith and ethics has become one of the most vigorously debated topics in theology.[1] Yet, over this same period, sermons that focus on the cross have become rare in many pulpits, particularly those of the traditionally "mainline" denominational churches. Preachers I talk with consider the death of Jesus crucially important, yet a surprising number admit that they find themselves at a loss for words to interpret its significance to twenty-first-century congregations. They believe that the long-ago, violent death of Jesus of Nazareth was integral to God's redeeming this broken world, but communicating that claim in a world filled with violence, often religiously motivated, is a challenge. Others, alert to the way certain traditional ideas of atonement have sometimes functioned in damaging ways for sufferers and abuse victims, are uneasy about using traditional language about sacrifice or saving death in the pulpit.

It would be inaccurate to claim that preaching on the cross has dwindled uniformly in every North American church tradition. In churches that retain the custom of regular catechetical preaching—for example, at Sunday evening services in some congregations of the Christian Reformed Church or Orthodox Presbyterian Church—doctrinal reflection on the meaning of the cross is not uncommon. In some African American church contexts, it is expected that the preacher will "lead the congregation to the cross" at the sermon's close, whatever its theme or text. In churches where the rhythms of the Christian year are scrupulously observed, the focus of lectionary and liturgy swings toward the cross at least in Holy Week. Yet, even in these contexts, many preachers tend to limit themselves to a brief narration of the events of Jesus' crucifixion or cautiously invoke a few well-worn turns of phrase that, truth be told, bear little relevance for younger generations of believers.[2] Congregations are often left to cobble together for themselves from liturgy and hymns some rudimentary understanding of the difference the cross makes.

In this book I invite preachers to explore the significant challenges that have suppressed preaching about the death of Jesus in many churches today. I hope not only to help preachers become more conversant with some of today's important theological debates about interpreting Jesus' death, but also to help them find fresh forms of speech that can demonstrate for twenty-first-century Christians the difference the cross makes in their faith and witness.

Many theologians would agree that failing to say *anything* from the pulpit about Jesus' death is a problem, but they disagree—often vigorously—about what *should* be said. Contemporary theologians working from many perspectives are concerned about the concrete effects of Christian doctrines on the lives of society's most vulnerable—those in particular who find themselves at the margins of social, political, and ecclesiastical power structures. For example, when sufferers and abuse victims believe that Jesus' death was divinely orchestrated violence and that the suffering of Jesus was intrinsically redemptive, the results can be disastrous. If, for example, it is implied that suffering is by definition meritorious, a victim's motivation to question or resist the conditions of their suffering, regardless of cause, can be undercut. Victims may accept the violence they suffer as inevitable if those in authority (be they government officials, ecclesial authority figures, or raging parents) assert that such violence is a necessary means to righteous ends. Critics of traditional atonement language warn that, if interpreting the cross as salvific has left in its wake legacies such as these, preachers ought to think twice before speaking too glibly of the cross as a divinely ordained, saving event.

Other theologians, however, argue that despite the risks involved, we cannot afford to fall silent on the subject of the cross. A diverse and growing cadre of thinkers (black, feminist, and postcolonialist theologians among them) are committed to reviving a theological tradition known as "theology of the cross," traceable to the work of Martin

Luther. Luther contrasted "theology of the cross" with "theology of glory."[3] A theology of glory attempts to domesticate the cross, turning it into a symbol that inspires devotion, but refusing to let it fundamentally shape Christian faith and practice. Luther contended that when a theology of glory takes over the church's imagination and practice, the church becomes self-aggrandizing, seeking worldly power and influence in the name of Christ. We must resist such a theology of glory, Luther insisted, and forthrightly embrace a "theology of the cross," which recognizes that God is indispensably revealed in the Crucified.

Contemporary theologians of the cross argue that the death of Jesus discloses for Christians their fundamental understanding of the nature of God and God's redemptive engagement with human experience. Failing to proclaim the cross as the "key signature" of God's redemptive presence to us ultimately bodes ill for society's most vulnerable, because only a church that lives under the cross will willingly recognize that it is to the margins, the place of risk, vulnerability, and "outsider" status, that Jesus leads us.[4]

In this book I take seriously both the concerns of those who stress the damage done by some of our cross talk and those who urge us to continue to set the cross at the center of our faith. Certainly some of our prevalent ways of interpreting Jesus' death have left damage in their wake. At the same time, I am convinced that the cross discloses in an indispensable way how God is redemptively engaged with the sin, suffering, and violence of our world. To speak again of the cross in their sermons, however, preachers today need fresh points of departure and fresh language equal to the task.

A BROADER LANGUAGE FOR SALVATION

Some preachers will leaf through this book in bewilderment, wondering what all the fuss is about. Preachers who find preaching about the death of Jesus today unproblematic and straightforward will find this book superfluous at best, wrongheaded at worst. My best hope is that curiosity may prompt a few of them to read on, anyway; but this book is not written mainly for them. This book is for their colleagues, no less faithful and no less concerned to preach the "whole counsel of God," who have found themselves stammering lately when it comes to interpreting Jesus' death. Some are uneasy with formulaic language about soul-salvation that does not reach those parishioners whose pressing question is whether God is redemptively engaged with their physical, emotional, and mental suffering. Preachers must speak of the cross to congregations exhausted by a barrage of news reports filled with war, disaster, and rampant injustice. This book is for preachers who, along with their congregations, wonder how to come to terms with a violent death that lies at the heart of their faith in a suffering, chaotic world, which sees all too much violence that claims to be sanctioned by God.

This book is also for preachers who sense a gap, or lack of fit, between the biblical text on one hand, and on the other hand the form and content of the atonement theories that they brought with them from seminary. To be sure, the Scriptures attest that the cross matters; but given the practical effects of traditional atonement theories among the oppressed, marginalized, and abused, more and more preachers today are in search of new ways to talk about the difference the cross makes. This book is for preachers who want to proclaim a cross-centered gospel in language that takes seriously both the biblical tradition and the social and cultural realities faced by those who occupy the pews.

I use the phrase "the saving significance of Jesus' death" rather than "atonement." This choice is deliberate.[5] Speaking of "the saving significance of Jesus' death" reflects an important shift in theological conversations about the cross in the last few decades. While "atonement theology" has been customary shorthand for better than two centuries to refer to all theological reflection on Jesus' death, the word "atonement" has to do specifically with the difference Jesus' death makes in divine-human estrangement caused by human sin. Today many theologians urge us to recognize that Jesus' death bears saving significance for the brokenness of the whole created order in a much broader sense: while the cross indeed reveals God's redemptive engagement with sin (which, furthermore, must be conceived in social as well as individual terms), it also reveals God's redemptive engagement with all that diminishes human life. Thus the saving news the cross discloses must have a bearing not only on sin but also on the great range of human suffering; it must make a saving difference in a world rife with violence from the bedroom to the battlefield.

REDEMPTION HERE AND NOW

The subtitle of this book requires some explaining. Why speak of preaching redemption "here and now"? Concrete social and cultural location makes a difference in all interpretation.[6] We always seek the good news of God's redemptive engagement with us from and for the particular places of our social, cultural, economic, and political existence—our "place."[7] We preachers do not preach the gospel in general; we want to discover with our congregations how the news of God's engagement with us in Jesus Christ makes a difference amid our community's particular experiences—the sorrows we bear, the fears that plague us, the responsibilities we carry. We preachers wrestle in our studies with the biblical witness, the pastoral ambiguities of our community's life, and the questions raised by each day's news, hastening at last from study to pulpit to declare what the God revealed in a man crucified and risen has to say to us, right here and right now.

The hermeneutical principle of preaching from and for a particular time and place resonates, in my judgment, with a perspective on interpreting Jesus' death suggested by David Kelsey. Kelsey urges us to speak of "imagining redemption." Instead of speaking in terms of "'understanding' or 'interpreting' or 'conceiving' redemption," Kelsey suggests, "imagining" helps us "respect the concrete particularity of the set of situations to which Jesus may make a redemptive difference."[8] The situations congregations face include not only sin and its effects, but also the realities of living in a world fraught with profound suffering, rampant injustice, and seemingly endless violence. We need to help our congregations imagine within these specific realities what God has done, is doing, and will do, to redeem. We seek to preach the saving significance of Jesus' death in ways that do not merely "inform," but also equip the congregation to move from sanctuary to street and there to discern the redeeming work of God.

FROM EXPLANATION TO EXPLORATION

My goal in this book is not to develop yet one more "theory" of atonement. This book will not satisfy those who are looking for a single master image that exhaustively explains the efficacy of Jesus' death, anticipating every situation and avoiding all the problems of the past. Several recent ventures along these lines are thought provoking and illuminating; but I proceed here in the conviction that no single paradigm, no matter how brilliantly conceived, can undergird all of our preaching on the death of Jesus. Instead of proposing any single theory—or, for that matter, any "theory" at all—I point to the evidence of the New Testament and argue that preachers today must draw on a diversity of "metaphors of redemption," deployed within concrete situations, to disclose what the cross reveals about God's redemptive engagement with us.

Cross talk in the New Testament is almost bafflingly *un*systematic and richly diverse. Biblical metaphors of redemption are evocative, yet unapologetically modest. No single metaphor provides a comprehensive, all-purpose explanation of the saving efficacy of Jesus' death or parses fine the "logic" or "mechanics" of salvation. It is telling that no single metaphor of redemption came to dominate New Testament discourse; and no early church council ever declared one metaphor or model of redemption more authoritative than the others. The multiplicity of metaphors that New Testament writers used is intentional; and this variety itself is a clue for contemporary preaching. Furthermore, those metaphors function in illuminating and disclosive ways precisely when drawn into lively relationship with particular situations. Metaphors of redemption function in relation to human experience like different wavelengths of light. Infrared light, "black" light, and other wavelengths beyond the visible spectrum disclose different features in a scene. Likewise, various metaphors of redemption turned loose amid the realities of our lives disclose different dynamics of divine redemption at work among us.

Our job as preachers, I suggest, is not to "explain" atonement in terms of comprehensive abstractions, but as I have said, to "imagine redemption" for particular situations. Thus our pulpit cross talk will be more pastoral than theoretical, and more evocative than comprehensive in its aims. It will have the texture of exploration rather than explanation, opening new imaginative trajectories of redemption rather than seeking closure and completeness.

This is not to say that theories of atonement have no legitimate role to play in a congregation's thinking about the cross. Theories of atonement are efforts at thinking out in systematic ways the implications of certain concepts and images associated with the death of Jesus. Every theory about the saving efficacy of Jesus' death can be thought of as elaborating a particular image or metaphor drawn from the tradition.[9] There is no reason why Christian believers should not be introduced to such modes of reflection in appropriate learning contexts and invited to wrestle with their implications. Yet, as helpful as it may be from time to time to reason our way through atonement theories, "downloading" them into sermons forces them into a role for which they are ill suited. I am persuaded that today's preachers instead need to become adept pastoral "poets" of the cross. Preaching about the difference Jesus' death makes is a lively, practical art. It requires us, like our New Testament forebears, to draw an array of metaphors of redemption into lively relationship with the concrete experiences of the people we address on Sunday morning, helping them recognize what God is doing, here and now.

CROSS TALK AND THE HORIZON OF DIVINE PROMISE IN PREACHING

The preacher's task of imagining redemption takes place against the larger horizon of *all* Christian preaching: announcing God's promise kept and being kept in Jesus Christ. God's promise kept is the re-creation of all things in the Word made flesh, crucified and risen. This is the fundamental, world-changing news, explicit or implicit, of every Christian sermon.

At the heart of Christian preaching lies the scandalous claim that God's promise to renew all things in accord with the divine will is inseparable from the long-ago death of a man called Jesus on a Roman cross. It is important to remember that there would have been *no impulse at all* to reinterpret in a positive manner this particular death by crucifixion if it were not for two particular, subsequent events. The first event that compelled Jesus' followers to radically reconsider their Jewish faith and to reassess Jesus' death was their experience of the risen Christ. Beginning on the third day after Jesus' execution, Jesus' disciples became persuaded that Jesus had been raised by God as the "firstborn" of God's promised new creation (Col. 1:15). The resurrection validated all Jesus had said, done, and undergone and required a thorough reassessment of (among other things) his ignominious death. A second event soon followed that further propelled the reinterpretation of Jesus' execution: gathered for prayer on the day of Pentecost, following the tumultuous Passover when Jesus was killed, his followers experienced the outpouring of the divine Spirit. This they recognized immediately and unmistakably as an eschatological sign, the fulfillment of promises like those in Joel 2. God's age-old promise to renew all things was kept and being kept, stunningly, through one who had been crucified. Early Christians had to grapple with the astounding possibility that not only the resurrection and the outpouring of the Spirit, but also Jesus' public humiliation on the cross was the very revelation of God and God's redeeming ways with the world.

The proclamation that Jesus' death is integral to God's redemption of the world stands at the center of all Christian preaching. The cross, far from being a temporary aberration in the career of God Incarnate, is the indispensable means of God's ongoing redemptive engagement with us and the disclosure of God's very nature. Preachers announce that God's promise is kept in Christ crucified and risen; and by this word proclaimed, God is making all things new.[10]

THE PLAN OF THE BOOK

In the first half of this book (chaps. 1–3), I make a case that the growing silence about the cross in preaching today not only *can* be broken, but also *must* be. In chapter 1 I explore the impasse many preachers confront when they consider speaking about the significance of Jesus' death in their sermons. First, they sense a gap between the forms of reflection on Jesus' death learned in seminary—generally in the form of atonement theories—and the kind of cross talk they actually find when they open the Bible to begin work on the upcoming sermon. Second, many are alert to the serious concerns raised by many black, feminist, and womanist theologians about certain forms of atonement thought and their practical effects. Pastors are not necessarily comfortable with leaving their congregations to piece together their understanding of the cross from random sources like Christian music or television preachers, but many find themselves at a loss for words about the death of Jesus.

I argue in chapters 2 and 3 that breaking this silence requires a two-pronged strategy. First, in chapter 2 I suggest that the kind of cross talk we actually find in the New Testament provides fruitful models for preachers to follow. Too often, we treat the New Testament strictly as a source book in soteriology. Yet what we find in the New Testament is a vast array of metaphorical images for redemption drawn into lively dialogue with the situations and experiences of the communities New Testament writers sought to address. Pastoral and poetic, metaphorical and evocative, New Testament cross talk provides powerful clues for preaching today.

However, finding new language to speak of the cross is only part of the task; preachers also need critically to engage what I call "cross talk gone wrong," distorted understandings of redemption that have taken hold in the imagination of some Christians. Chapter 3, therefore, deals with the fact that some ways of speaking about Jesus' death have not promoted liberation, but have reinforced unhealthy forms of piety that valorize self-denigration and make a virtue of suffering, self-imposed or passively endured. Before new ways of "imagining" redemption can take hold, preachers have to clear away misunderstandings and distortions. Since cross talk has malfunctioned in the past particularly for women, especially those who have suffered abuse, women preachers have been acutely sensitive to these dynamics. Many examples in this chapter are drawn, then, from the preaching of women.

Chapters 4 and 5 encourage preachers to connect their cross talk with two dimensions of human experience that cry out for redemptive address: suffering and violence. In Chapter 4, I develop several metaphors that can be drawn into creative dialogue with the on-the-ground realities of suffering, individual and collective. Chapter 5 explores resources on how we can proclaim the saving significance of Jesus' death for a world of violence, doing so in ways that challenge rather than sanction violence.

Chapter 6 is somewhat different from the previous two chapters; here, I invite preachers to consider a particularly enduring metaphor in Christian reflection on the cross from the church's beginnings, the metaphor of sacrifice. Sacrifice, perhaps best regarded as a web of metaphors rather than a single image or paradigm, has become controversial in some circles today. Yet it has had staying power in Christian reflection on redemption, especially as a way of understanding our redemption from sin and guilt. I therefore discuss the problems and possibilities of sacrifice, and how new ways of understanding sacrifice open up, in turn, our understanding of sin and redemption.

In the closing chapter (7), I consider how we can make our preaching on the death of Jesus relevant to its liturgical and cultural context. Careful liturgical choices, as well as utilizing opportunities for congregational reflection on the words prayed and sung, can help reinforce fresh visions of redemption, rather than undercut them. In addition to testing the liturgical relevance of our cross talk, we need to ask questions about its cultural relevance: Can we construct fresh metaphors beyond those explicitly found in the biblical tradition? A discussion of this question draws the book to a close.

Throughout the book, I have included examples from published sermons that illustrate the strategies I am commending here. In chapters 4–7 these sermon discussions appear under the title "Preaching Notes," and in those chapters the sermon discussions are coupled with my discussion of specific metaphors of redemption that disclose God's saving work in particular ways. Sermons that focus on the saving significance of the cross or help listeners think carefully about the ways we have traditionally made sense of Jesus' death are not terribly plentiful, especially in the last twenty years; but they are there to be found. I am grateful for all I have learned from the preachers whose work is cited in this book, and many others as well.

After the final chapter, readers will find an appendix in chart form, which indicates where, for each year of the three-year New Revised Common Lectionary cycle, texts can be found that make reference to Jesus' death. I hope that lectionary and nonlectionary preachers alike will find this to be a useful resource as they plan their preaching, but I also hope they will not limit themselves to these texts. Others that the lectionary cycle misses also need to be preached. Old Testament texts about sacrifice come to mind as especially relevant.

Down the ages Christians have declared that God has established the human future precisely in One crucified and risen. God's promise to renew all things was inscribed in flesh and blood at the cross. In a world where human beings find themselves entangled at every level of experience in forces that destroy human well-being, both as perpetrators and as victims, this news could not be more crucial. So why are preachers finding themselves at a loss for words on the subject of the cross today? How can the silence be broken? It is to these questions that I turn next.

1

At a Loss for Words

Why Preachers Are Falling Silent about the Cross

Mel Gibson's grueling cinematic portrayal of Jesus' final hours, *The Passion of the Christ,* was released to record crowds in the spring of 2004. It created such a sensation that television newscasts, cable features, and radio talk shows were abuzz with discussions about the death of Jesus. Theologians of every stripe, more accustomed to dimly lit library corners than floodlit television studios, found themselves facing the cameras to opine on the atonement. Emblazoned on *Time* magazine's April 12 cover that spring was the question "Why Did Jesus Die?"[1] With admiral brevity author David Van Biema managed to help *Time*'s readers understand what all the fuss was about. Van Biema described the three standard theories about the atoning significance of Jesus' death—as a payment for sin-incurred debt (its most popular version in North America being penal substitutionary atonement theory), as divine triumph over evil (ransom theory), and as a compelling example of suffering love (moral influence theory).

Van Biema's most remarkable achievement may have been to enlighten thousands of already professing Christians about a topic that, truth be told, many knew very little. Van Biema reported that, apart from a few well-worn but marginally understood phrases such as "Jesus died for our sins," many Christians today are stumped when it comes to articulating in any coherent way the meaning of Jesus' death for their faith and practice. "The large proportion of Christians," he wrote, admitted they "really didn't think of Jesus' death much at all" until the topic was brought to the forefront of public debate by the release of Gibson's film. This, concludes Van Biema, "suggests a Christianity with a large hole in it where, at the very least, some thought should go."[2] If such a "hole" exists in the day-to-day experience of many Christians, one might also expect to find such a "hole" in the week-to-week preaching heard in many pulpits. Indications are that there indeed is such a gap, and it is gradually widening. More and more preachers seem to be lapsing into silence on the subject of how and why Jesus' death has significance for Christian faith, worship, and witness.

A couple of years ago, I brought up my hunch about this growing silence in a continuing education seminar for preachers. The participants—twenty-two pastors of all ages from a range of denominations—readily acknowledged that the falloff in sermons on the cross was not a figment of my imagination. Furthermore, they were relieved that someone was finally bringing up this difficult subject. Only a couple could recall preaching a sermon on the death of Jesus over the past two or three years. Many expressed surprise at how little they were actually saying about the cross from the pulpit. While several reported *narrating* the passion story on the occasional Good Friday or Palm/Passion Sunday, exploring with their congregations the saving significance of the death of Jesus was not a part of their homiletical repertoire.

It was not that these preachers did not think of Jesus' crucifixion as significant for Christian faith. It was clear that everyone in the room regarded Jesus' death as central to the Christian story; most considered it essential, in fact, to an adequate Christian understanding of God's engagement with the powers of sin, evil, and death. So why were they avoiding the subject? One pastor seemed to speak for many in the room: "I know a little about the debates in theology about traditional atonement theories, especially the penal substitution type, and the way glorifying the cross becomes a problem for victims of abuse—and I don't want to go there. But even if that weren't true—are we supposed to *preach* atonement theories? I've tried; almost everyone out in the pews glazes over. Sure, I worry about what I'm leaving unsaid. But, frankly, at this point I don't know what to say or how to say it."

This preacher's remarks indicate at least two significant problems that preachers face when they consider preaching about the saving significance of Jesus' death. First, many are alert to widespread concerns among theologians about the impact of certain popular and influential ideas of atonement on Christian believers. These concerns focus on the way ideas about sacrifice and suffering are played out in the belief systems of sufferers and abuse victims. If Jesus' suffering is portrayed as redemptive, and sufferers are urged to identify with Jesus, suffering and the abuse that causes suffering become a sacred necessity, not a wrong to be exposed and challenged.

Second, there are good reasons to wonder whether theories of atonement as such, whatever their particular claims, ought to find their way into the pulpit. Over the last three decades, homiletical theory and practice has taken a decisive turn toward the biblical text itself as a guide for both the form and content of sermons. However, as more and more preachers struggle to take seriously not only the message of the text but also its communication strategies, they find it hard to reconcile the ways the New Testament speaks about the cross with the form and content of atonement theories learned in the seminary classroom. Atonement theories, instead of helping preachers illuminate the cross for their congregations, have sometimes felt more like an insurmountable barrier. Reviewing the basic forms that atonement theory has taken is an important step, then, toward getting a handle on the issues preachers face when it comes to preaching about the cross.

THREE THEORIES OF ATONEMENT: BLESSING OR BANE?

A majority of pastors are heir to some version of a three-theory summary of the saving significance of Jesus' death, identified by Gustav Aulén in his influential 1931 monograph, *Christus Victor*.[3] Aulén's aim in this work was to argue for the largely neglected "ransom" interpretation of atonement, which builds on themes of captivity and deliverance; but just as important for twentieth-century discussions of atonement, Aulén reorganized the variety of available interpretations of Jesus' death into three basic categories of atonement theology: (1) satisfaction, or "objective" theories; (2) moral influence, or "subjective" views; and (3) ransom theory, which Aulén regarded as the "classic" view of atonement and most characteristic of the church's earliest reflection on the death of Jesus.[4]

The satisfaction view and its cognates (including the penal substitutionary view, solidified for North American theology in the nineteenth century by Charles Hodge of Princeton) Aulén designated "objective" theories. These interpret Jesus' death as a divinely initiated saving event necessary to satisfy the requirements of divine justice and effect change in God's disposition toward sinners. The moral influence, or "subjective," view accents the effect of the death of Jesus on human beings who are drawn to God by a profound demonstration of divine love. Aulén argued for the superiority of ransom theory, which, in his view, exhibits both objective and subjective elements and avoids the weaknesses of the other approaches.

In the West, particularly in churches of the Reformed tradition, the most influential theories are of the satisfaction type. The term "satisfaction" itself comes from the work of Anselm of Canterbury, who interpreted the significance of Jesus' death within the framework of his work on the doctrine of incarnation, *Cur Deus homo (Why God Became Man)*. Anselm drew on the medieval, feudal social context of his time, in which social obligations were based on rank, with honor due those of higher social standing, and reparations being required where due honor had not been rendered. According to satisfaction theory, humankind owes satisfaction to God for our offense against God's honor. We must pay the debt, but we cannot; only one whose resources are infinite can render the satisfaction due to God. Thus God became human in Jesus Christ and rendered satisfaction to God's self, achieving on humanity's behalf the needed reparation and the restoration of divine-human relationship.

The Reformers and their theological successors elaborated Anselm's satisfaction view in various ways appropriate to their times. Calvin, trained as a lawyer, recast the saving effect of the cross in terms of the legal context with which he was familiar, bringing into the picture a concept of sin as penal liability and incorporating into his atonement thought a distinctly retributive understanding of justice.[5] Calvin's successors, the Protestant scholastics, further developed Calvin's basic ideas (albeit not always in helpful ways). This juridically based family of interpretations is generally designated "penal substitutionary" atonement theory.

Satisfaction theory and its offshoots have had a pervasive influence on North American Protestantism. What comes to expression today in popular hymnody and print media, however, is not pure satisfaction theory. It exhibits many elements of penal substitutionary atonement thought, although it often lacks Calvin's Trinitarian accents or subtlety of insight. Anselm's satisfaction theory has also heavily influenced Catholic atonement theology, although it has never been elevated to the status of dogma.

Peter Abelard, a younger contemporary of Anselm, found Anselm's view, with its portrayal of God as unable to forgive without the satisfaction of God's honor, unthinkable. Abelard could not imagine that God should be pleased with, or find satisfactory or necessary, the death of

God's own innocent Son, no matter what the reason. Abelard held that it was *humanity* that needed reconciliation, not God; and Jesus' handing over of himself to death out of love for humanity was intended to so move humanity that men and women would be drawn closer to God by it, thus ending divine-human estrangement.

Christus Victor theory builds on themes of captivity and deliverance. The theory assumes cosmic struggle between God and the forces of evil (in many early versions, specifically the devil), with sinful humanity held captive to evil powers. Christ appears to fall prey to death's clutches, yet ultimately overcomes the devil, taking humanity with him. In some versions, Jesus is the ransom God pays to set humans free from bondage; but because Jesus is "disguised" in human flesh, Satan does not realize his "prize" is stronger than he, and in the resurrection, Christ escapes Satan's clutches, leaving the devil empty-handed. A variation on the same theme envisions a specifically military paradigm: Jesus is the warrior who wins a victory over Satan and all evil powers, emancipating humanity.[6]

The three-theory scheme for thinking about the efficacy of Jesus' death has proved to be useful for many a seminary student cramming for the theology midterm. But as I have noted, it has come under attack in recent decades. First, the history of Christian reflection on the significance of the cross is far more complex than Aulén's scheme gave us to believe. For centuries after Jesus' death, theologians used a wide array of images to convey the efficacy of the cross—images that resist resolution into anything like three "types." Nancy J. Duff speaks for many: "Most scholars agree that Aulén's categories are simplistic and that his bias for Christus Victor leads to unfair presentations of opposing viewpoints."[7] Furthermore, speaking in terms of just three theories tends to gloss over important differences between related but fundamentally different theories within Aulén's trio of categories, such as Anselmian satisfaction theory and the much-later penal substitutionary model, or between these views and other "objective" views based on concepts of sacrifice in the Old Testament. The three-theory scheme is simply not rich enough or diverse enough to fairly present the breadth of perspectives that have informed Christian faith and practice over the centuries. Peter Schmiechen, for example, has clearly identified no less than ten distinct "theories" of atonement that have claimed a significant place in Christian reflection on the cross.[8]

A second difficulty is that the legacy of these theories as the basis for Christian understanding of the cross has been mixed, to say the least. Third, whether "theories," as such, can provide a useful basis for preaching and teaching at all is debatable. It is to these problems that we turn next.

THE CROSS, SUFFERING, AND ABUSE:
RECENT ATONEMENT DEBATES

For some theologians, the pressing concern is not Aulén's overly narrow menu of atonement theories, but the observable, practical effects of these doctrines on the faith and behavior of Christians, particularly sufferers and victims of abuse. Taking the lead in critiques of classic atonement theories have been black, feminist, womanist, and postcolonialist theologians. What these theologians have in common is a methodological commitment to assessing theology from particular, concrete social locations, stressing the social location of those at the margins of social and political power (and at the margins, as well, of the bodies that produce and "authorize" theology). They argue that the "meaning" of our theological claims consists of more than the interrelations among the words we use. The meaning of a theological idea includes the *effects* of disseminating that idea among persons in specific situations. Testing the adequacy of any atonement doctrine requires more than checking its internal consistency or explanatory comprehensiveness; one must also ask specific questions about the social, political, and even economic effects of turning its claims loose in a concrete historical setting.[9] Pastors and theologians who began examining the effects of traditional atonement ideas among real people, especially those who have suffered domestic or political violence, made some alarming discoveries.

They discovered that victims of abuse were not being empowered by the Christian message of the cross to resist or flee situations of abuse. In fact, anecdotal evidence established beyond any reasonable doubt that far too often, victims had been taught by pastors, Bible study leaders, and well-meaning Christian friends to "rejoice" in their suffering and endure abuse as Jesus did; to make this point, they had drawn precisely upon ideas about the redemptive nature of Jesus' suffering and death. Theologian Rebecca Parker tells the story of an abuse sufferer, Lucia, who came to her seeking counseling. Lucia had been told by her pastor that she must not leave her husband no matter how much he beat her; instead, she should bear her suffering "gladly" as a way of identifying with Jesus on the cross.[10]

We are less inclined than ever to overlook or take lightly such stories. As Ellen Charry writes:

> Many in our own day are troubled by a type of Christian piety that finds suffering redemptive and approves of blind obedience to authority, possibly exemplified by Christ's obedience to the Father. And the notion that the Father handed the Son over to death seems to condone cruelty on the part of God and, by extension, on the part of persons in positions of authority.[11]

When, through appeals to the redemptive effects of the cross, women are counseled to return to abusive spouses, children are told to keep quiet and cover up the bruises inflicted by raging parents, and the politically and socially persecuted are taught to endure their lot instead of resist—then something has gone terribly wrong. Instead of delivering victims from life-destroying forces, some interpretations of the cross seem to deliver victims into the hands of their abusers.

Feminist and womanist critics of Western atonement traditions identify as especially troubling the power dynamics between the first and second persons of the Godhead implied in some versions of atonement theory. The problem is that these dynamics can appear to lend an aura of the sacred to power that asserts itself by domination. Wrathful dominators and submissive victims seem to be playing out a sacred drama. Suffering and death in general tend to be dangerously sacralized.[12] Womanist theologian Delores Williams has criticized Western atonement theology in particular from the perspective of the concrete life experiences of black women under conditions of slavery and subsequently as primary suppliers of menial household labor in white society. Black women, Williams reminds us, played a surrogate role for white women under the conditions of slavery. They often reared the children of white women and, most sadly, were conscripted into serving the sexual demands of white masters. Against the backdrop of this historical legacy, says Williams, "it is . . . fitting and proper for black women to ask whether the image of a surrogate-God has salvific power for black women, or whether this image supports and reinforces the exploitation that has accompanied their experience with surrogacy."[13]

We are ethically obliged to attend to the ways our theological language can be misconstrued and misapplied. It is to their credit that preachers who recognize that traditional cross talk has promoted such situations hesitate before they step to the pulpit to speak of Jesus' death as redemptive. When atonement theories imply that a dominating, wrathful parent-God forces a guiltless child to suffer horrible abuse and death—and not for any wrongs done, but as a stand-in for others—the implications are so deeply unacceptable that such theories must be discarded. Some find the effects of atonement thinking so appalling that they urge us to give up any attempt to connect redemption with the cross. Instead, they argue, we must articulate visions of redemption that make Jesus' life, not his death, the point of departure for a worthy understanding of the redemptive significance of Jesus.[14] Whether this radical change is plausible is a question that we will take up shortly; but given all that is at stake, the impulse is not hard to understand.

ARE ATONEMENT THEORIES THE RIGHT FOUNDATION FOR PREACHING?

The damaging effects of some atonement ideas on Christian belief and behavior need to be taken seriously. But this is not the only difficulty preachers encounter when they try to interpret Jesus' death in their sermons. A particularly urgent question for preachers is how to negotiate the obvious difference in form and content between traditional theories of atonement and the cross talk preachers find on the pages of the New Testament. There is no shortage of biblical texts that allude to the cross in the New Testament; however, theories of atonement are decidedly *not* what we find there.

New Testament cross talk is largely unsystematic. This is not to say that New Testament writers, particularly Paul, did not think coherently about the meaning of the cross. Rather, what guided New Testament writers was not so much a concern to organize their thought into a comprehensive system, but a desire to address the news of redemption to human needs in particular settings. In other words, the wide array of lively, diverse images we find in the New Testament was evoked by the particular challenges local congregations were facing in the world of early Christian mission. Writers chose images because they were contextually relevant and allowed persons in particular circumstances to "imagine" the redemptive difference Jesus' death made within their concrete experience. Images from the household and battlefield, the marketplace and the temple court, were drawn into a metaphorical relationship to Jesus' death.

Inherent in metaphor (as we shall see in chap. 2) is a creative imprecision of fit between two ideas or visual images. Accordingly, none of the images New Testament writers employed were intended as complete and exhaustive replicas of the dynamics of redemption disclosed in the cross. Instead, they functioned as evocative lenses to help congregations imagine God's redemptive activity amid such diverse experiences as the reinterpretation of traditional religious practices and texts, the expansion of the church into unexpected cultures and contexts, the new freedom of expression among women, and the realities of poverty, suffering, persecution, temptation, and community conflict.

Metaphorical diversity was the rule in Christian preaching and teaching for centuries, although some metaphors were evidently favored in certain eras of the church's life (for example, sacrifice in the first and second centuries, and the image of deliverance of captives for several centuries thereafter). Notably, there was never any attempt to settle upon a single, normative account of the saving significance of Jesus' death comparable to the consensus agreements achieved at the councils of Nicaea and Chalcedon regarding the Trinity and the divine-human nature of Christ. No single metaphor was embraced as the master key to explaining the saving significance of Jesus' death.

THEOLOGY AS PRACTICAL WISDOM

There are reasons, says Charry, why preachers sense a gap between the forms of theological reflection they learned in seminary and cross talk in the New Testament. The problem derives in part, Charry suggests, from a gradual shift that took place over centuries in the accepted norms of rationality and means of persuasion that have governed theological discourse.[15]

For New Testament writers as well as for early Christian teachers and preachers for many subsequent centuries, theology was a form of *sapientia*, or practical wisdom. Theology-as-*sapientia* was intended to form Christian believers in the love of God and neighbor, and theological reflection on Christian claims was shaped to that end. Theology, assumed early Christian thinkers, was meant to evoke confidence and faithful living in believers. Thus both its content and means of persuasion aimed not at systematization, but at positive formational effect.[16] Writing on Augustine's theology of the cross, for example, John Cavadini makes the telling observation that it is difficult to derive a *systematic* sense of Augustine's thinking about the significance of Jesus' death from his sermons:

> [Augustine's] comments about the cross itself are scattered amid his
> treatises and letters, sermons and commentaries, and need to be
> combed out and sifted through, connected and expanded, if we are
> to have anything like an Augustinian doctrine of the cross . . . It is in
> his sermons that we find the most frequent and most colorful refer-
> ences to the cross itself, though frequently they are left undeveloped
> and we are left looking for further explanation.[17]

Augustine's homiletical cross talk, in other words, was not intended as
a fully developed theology of the cross; rather, he used such arresting
images as the mousetrap, boat, and "the tree of silly fruit" (!) to sometimes lure, sometimes startle his listeners into an imaginative appreciation of the redemptive effects of the cross amid the realities of their
daily experience.

But in later centuries, particularly as new understandings of rationality came to be valued by the emerging intellectual culture of the late
eleventh century, theological reflection found itself under pressure to
meet new criteria of reason. With the Enlightenment came increasing
pressure for theology to prove itself as a "science" entitled to a place in
university studies. Theology-as-*sapientia* (wisdom) came more and
more to be displaced by theology-as-*scientia* (science). "Reason," writes
Charry, "as a tool of absolute knowledge took on a life of its own that
bent in the direction of denying the intelligibility of Christian claims
unless knowledge of God was empirically or rationally demonstrable."[18]

Theology-as-*scientia*, explains Charry, became preoccupied not with
the positive formational effects of theological discourse but with concerns for explanatory comprehensiveness, rationalistic and empirical
warrants, and strictly consistent conceptual structure.[19] This shift in the
form and aims of theological reflection is perhaps nowhere more evident than in atonement theology. Edward Farley, who traces a similar
history of the transformation of theology's form and aims, agrees that
theology lost its character as practical wisdom and became more and
more a theoretical science. To the extent that the "practical wisdom"
emphasis in theology survived at all, it did so in severely truncated form,
as ministerial "technology" for pastors.[20]

The cross talk we encounter in the pages of the New Testament fits
the theology-as-*sapientia* model. Unlike the atonement theories that
form part of the staple theological diet of many seminary students,
which were developed with strict attention to canons of internal consistency and explanatory comprehensiveness, the form and content of
New Testament writing on the cross is pastoral and poetic. New Testa-

ment writers' efforts to illuminate the saving significance of the death of Jesus were formed and informed by the materials at hand, responsive to the situations and purposes for which they preached and wrote, and intended to evoke imagination, vision, and faithful Christian witness amid adversity. Preachers who want to find their pulpit voices again on the subject of the cross can begin, I suggest, by simply paying close attention to New Testament cross talk in all its rhetorical diversity and pastoral depth.

This is not to say that atonement theories as such have no place in the work of the preacher. They do—but that place may not be the pulpit itself. Peter Schmiechen contends that the purpose of atonement theories "is fundamentally evangelical in nature, . . . to draw the listener/reader into the saving power of Christ," but admits that atonement theories "may not always appear in the form of sermons." I would add that they almost *never* do—and should not. Their role in shaping the content of our preaching is best thought of as indirect, as an important tool to help preachers think critically about the very matters that critics of the tradition have brought to our attention: the theological and practice-shaping implications of claims we make in preaching.[21]

WHY PREACH ABOUT THE CROSS?

A question we have to face head-on at this point, however, is whether to continue preaching about the cross at all. The damaging effects of certain atonement ideas for some Christians are too obvious to ignore. Might the most trenchant critics of atonement theologies be right after all? Might it be best, as some suggest, to understand Jesus' death as a lamentable tragedy—the consequence of living faithfully, but without redemptive significance? Is the growing silence about the cross in contemporary preaching actually a step in the right direction?

A surprisingly diverse group of contemporary theologians—black, feminist, womanist, and postcolonialist theologians among them—are convinced that the church cannot afford to lose touch with the cross. Working from many different sociocultural perspectives—North and Central American, Asian and African—they affirm unanimously that coming to terms with the cross is indispensable if we are going to understand how God enters redemptively into our varied human experience. They suggest that we need to reacquaint ourselves with what is sometimes called the "thin tradition" of "theology of the cross," a perspective on the cross that originates in the work of Martin Luther. With Luther, modern-day "theologians of the cross" are convinced that the cross must in fact remain the "key signature" that governs our interpretation of Christian conviction, worship, and witness.

The locus classicus for Luther's "theology of the cross" is theses 16 through 21 of the *Disputation* that Luther presented at Heidelberg in 1518.[22] Luther there outlines a series of fundamental contrasts between "theology of the cross" and "theology of glory." *Theologia crucis,* or theology of the cross, said Luther, "comprehends the visible and manifest things of God seen through suffering and the cross."[23] It recognizes God's presence in places and experiences of powerlessness, vulnerability, and suffering. Luther contended that theology shaped fundamentally by the cross is the only defense against what he called a spurious *theologia gloriae,* or "theology of glory," which eschews weakness and vulnerability and instead seeks dominion and success in the name of God. Luther contended that the apparatus of ecclesiastical power in his day was the quintessential expression of "theology of glory," exerting oppressive control over the souls and bodies of the faithful and living off their submission and poverty.

Today's theologians of the cross share the conviction that God is indispensably revealed in the dying of Jesus.[24] Feminist Lutheran theologian Deanna A. Thompson underscores that "what is at stake in operating as a cross or glory theologian, according to Luther, is nothing less than an accurate representation of reality."[25] God does not stand aloof from the cross in any sense, says Luther, overseeing or tolerating the outworking of the necessary machinery of redemption. Rather, "precisely where God seems least likely to be—in the shocking, shameful event of the cross—there God is, 'hidden in the suffering.' God's revelation is hidden *sub contrario* . . . within God's own strange and alien work."[26] Fundamentally, "theology of the cross" is a statement that the mystery of God, as well as all that it means to be given over to God, is revealed as Jesus suffers the pains of death at the cross. In a theology of the cross perspective, as opposed to a theology of glory, the cross is not an interruption of the career of God Incarnate—a regrettable but necessary transaction to deal with the obstacle of sin. Rather, the cross embodies the full presence of God, in and with death-doomed creation. God makes the fate of corrupt, beloved humanity and all creation God's own, in order to make God's life its own. God's own being is joined to creation's violent, deadly fate and, by undergoing its fate, alters its destiny. Every thought about God, every form of Christian praxis, and every act of worship directed toward God is radically recalibrated when God's true "glory" is understood not as a capacity to remain aloof from sin and evil, but as the divine passion to undergo the deadliness of the enslavement of humanity and all creation to evil so as to bring about the glory, the communion, that is creation's aim and possibility.

In the North American context in particular, the temptation is ever present to assign the cross a limited theological role, mainly connected with sin. Treating the cross this way can make it seem little more than an aberration or footnote within a theology that leans toward triumphalism. Theologian Douglas John Hall argues that the North American tendency to resist the cross as the point of departure for Christian faith and practice has deep historical roots. As scientific knowledge and technological invention burgeoned in the mid-nineteenth century, Western culture was buoyed by confidence in the promises of human technological progress and scientific mastery. As the church struggled to retain its credibility and the allegiance of its members, particularly wealthy entrepreneurs, it made a seemingly small but significant adjustment more rhetorical than deliberately theological. Subtly but significantly, the church negotiated what Hall calls "the elimination of the negative."[27] By the late nineteenth and early twentieth centuries, theological reflection about the cross was simply displaced in the theological academy by more spirited interest in Jesus' life and ministry. While the cross continued to function as a powerful symbol in the conversion-oriented piety of the frontier revival-influenced churches—a trend still reflected in the hymnody we have inherited from that period—the crucifixion no longer functioned any more as the profound theological center from which North American theology as a whole derived its understanding of God and the human condition.

By the mid-twentieth century, the situation was different in Europe, impacted not only physically and economically but also theologically by the devastation of two world wars. There, Jürgen Moltmann and others urged a stunned church to reconsider its theology in the "key signature" of the cross. Meanwhile, North America enjoyed a postwar population and prosperity boom. The spirit of the age was optimistic; and talk about the cross tended to be limited to matters of personal sin and individual forgiveness. David Van Biema speaks ruefully in his *Time* article of "American Christianity's ongoing romance with a friendly, helpful, personal Jesus, which has made detailed discussion of his violent death an increasingly difficult pulpit pitch."[28]

As their primary point of religious orientation, many North Americans prefer either the life of Jesus as ethical example or the resurrection of Christ as triumphal denial of death rather than the cross. Douglas John Hall writes:

> The theology of glory, in whatever guise it assumes, is invariably tempted to be a theology of sight, not faith; finality, not hope; and power, not love. The "thin tradition" [of the cross] throughout the ages of Christendom has often been marginalized, often wholly displaced, by the great triumph song of imperial religion. But it has never been without its representatives.[29]

Hall argues that Christian faith, worship, and public witness are profoundly changed if the point of departure for theological reflection is the cross. The result is a way of being in the world that is fragile and vulnerable, embodying with Christ the at-risk, saving passion of God, bent on revealing God's new creation and challenging the powers of the old age, exposed to the dark heart of violence. As Hall puts it,

> The faith that emanates from this cross is a faith that enables its disciples to follow the crucified God into the heart of the world's darkness, into the very kingdom of death, and to look for light that shines *in* the darkness, the life that is given beyond the baptismal brush with death—and only there.[30]

A theology of glory keeps asserting itself in Christianity today, as it always has, refusing such fragility and vulnerability by insisting that because Jesus "paid it all" we are somehow *exempt* from serious, potentially deadly, engagement with the darkness and violence of the world. Yet Jesus promised the way of the death-dealing cross to those who would share his life. The vulnerability of a theology of the cross remains threatening to a church and culture bent on success as the validation of its faith. Today's church can too easily wed its fortunes to a secular ideal of self-promotion and a sense of entitlement, forgetting its vocation to identify with the Crucified in all things.

Theology of the cross, says Hall, represents "a thin tradition that [has] tried to proclaim the possibility of hope without shutting its eyes to the data of despair."[31] If the Three in One is fully present in the crucifixion—willingly, bodily subject to suffering and evil—then Christianity cannot merely stand by and wring its hands as victims fall. The church's place is not at a distance from suffering, sufferers, and the depredations of abusive power, expressing its regret that those victims may not have heard the gospel. It is *among* the victims, where Christ himself is found.

It is striking that a revival of interest in the cross as centerpiece of theological reflection and Christian witness is taking hold where we might least expect it today. While many feminist theologians regard the cross as a potentially dangerous symbol for women, others like Deanna Thompson say that the cross is essential, in fact, to constructing liberating forms of Christian praxis (including preaching) in today's world. In fact, Thompson suggests that feminist theology and Luther's "theology of the cross" have far more in common than we might suppose: both can be understood as "reforming" traditions that have emerged in the church in order to expose oppressive undercurrents in the tradition and liberate Christians from life-diminishing beliefs and practices.[32]

Similarly, contemporary postcolonialist theologians of Central America and Africa are embracing the cross in new ways. An earlier generation of liberation theologians, decrying the effects of colonialism upon vast regions of Africa and Central America, saw the cross as the emblem of imperial conquest and the subjugation of peoples. Today, postcolonialist voices are part of the conversation about new possibilities in a cross-centered theology like Luther's. The cross, rightly understood, declares theologian Leonardo Boff, stands not as the rallying symbol of oppression but as the "judgment" and "moment of truth . . . of all human undertakings."[33] In postcolonial settings, theology of the cross as Luther understood it breaks down theological solipsism and self-absorption, whatever form it may take. On one hand, the cross calls into question Western hegemony over theological reflection; on the other, it challenges any tendency within local, situation-specific theologies to shut out all views but the community's own, so that anything alien to local interests is ignored.[34] Theology of the cross is humbly open to any and all "others."

Luther's theology of the cross is being embraced by some African American theologians as well. John Nunes describes his experience of undertaking ministry on the "raw, rough, and raging streets of North Philadelphia." Needing refuge at times from the relentless life-destroying violence and drug trafficking, the noise and the burned-out buildings, Nunes would sit in a Lutheran church (since destroyed by fire) where the words "Hail cross, our only hope" were inscribed in Latin on the altar-spanning arch. Nunes writes:

> Even amid a decaying and death-dealing neighborhood, I discovered consolation in the God-man whose death stands as a sign of hope against all death. For the kind of death that eventually kills us

physically, for the deaths of the flesh we must die daily in the spirit, for the killers that threaten and frighten, for urban horrors that make life a living hell, this symbol of the death of Jesus Christ faces all death squarely, overcomes death, and becomes a sign of hope— the cross means Christ's death absorbs all death and dying.[35]

I agree with these contemporary theologians of the cross that the only theology that makes any saving sense in a world of widespread suffering and violence is one that demonstrates God's deep and decisive engagement with the deathliness of much of human experience. At the cross— and only, finally, at the cross—do we come face to face with God undergoing death to defeat all that is deadening and deadly.

SPEAKING AGAIN OF THE CROSS

The cross matters, and preachers need to reclaim its central place in preaching so that it may reclaim its place, as well, in Christian witness. The witness of the church for centuries has been that Christians know God as indispensably disclosed in the Crucified. Allowing the cross to slip to the margins of Christian preaching, say today's theologians of the cross, poses dangers for the church—particularly the churches of North America and Europe, who are tempted by a secularized "gospel" of success and self-fulfillment. We need to empower twenty-first-century Christians to construct their faith, their worship, and their public witness according to the "key signature" of the cross by preaching sermons that help them envision the difference the cross makes amid the realities of their life experiences.

Preaching about the cross today is a twofold task, both critical and constructive. It is just as important to clear away false understandings of redemption as it is to help congregations find more fruitful ways of "imagining redemption" for their own lives and in the wider world. Nearly every congregation has some sound ideas about the significance of the cross. When this is true, the preacher can affirm this. Yet the difficulties we have touched on briefly in this chapter are real ones. Sometimes false and damaging ideas—for example, notions that suffering is intrinsically redemptive—have gained a toehold in congregational imagination and personal piety. False ideas about the meaning of Jesus' death need to be challenged.

Homiletician Leonora Tubbs Tisdale describes five ways that a sermon may interact with congregational thinking in order to affirm, challenge, stretch, or rebuild imagination. Tisdale suggests that a sermon may (1) affirm right imagination, (2) stretch partially correct imagination, (3) reorder disordered priorities, (4) seek to displace altogether existing imaginative constructs; or (5) introduce completely fresh ideas and visions.[36] Tisdale's five preaching tasks are helpful as we reconsider what it will take to restore cross talk to preaching today. Certainly, the first, second, and fifth approaches—affirming sound ideas, stretching those that tend in the right direction, and introducing fresh and productive ones—are indispensable. But equally important are the third and fourth tasks. Disordered ideas need to be sorted out; and some ideas are so flawed that the preacher will need to challenge them outright.

The next two chapters lay the groundwork for an approach to preaching on the death of Jesus that attends to both its critical and constructive aspects. In the next chapter I explore the cross talk we find in the New Testament as a model, both rhetorical and theological, for contemporary cross talk. New Testament cross talk, it turns out, is indeed interpretation of Jesus' death "here and now." This particularity, in the past often regarded as an obstacle to be overcome in interpretation, is a significant clue for preachers whose aim is to help their congregations discern the dynamics of redemption from and for concrete, present experience. New Testament cross talk is local, pastoral speech, aimed at answering to the specifics of particular cultures, locations, and critical experiences. The New Testament suggests that a rich diversity of metaphors can be drawn into relationship with a congregation's concrete realities to disclose how the God made known in the Crucified is redemptively engaged with our real lives today. Rhetorically, its multiple metaphors seem to be designed not so much to "explain" the "mechanics" of redemption in an exhaustive way, but to help Christians look through a variety of lenses, none of them final or complete, to discern the dynamics of God's redemptive engagement with them. Theologically, New Testament cross talk aims at changed lives as early Christians sought the shape of faithfulness to God's new order amid conflict and suffering.

In chapter 3 my focus shifts to the preacher's critical task. Black, feminist, womanist, and postcolonialist theologians are rightly concerned when society's most vulnerable are led to believe that God wills violence and suffering, or that suffering is intrinsically redemptive and should therefore be mutely accepted. Preachers must take on the task in their preaching of clearing away "false imagination." Here, after surveying the problems theologians have identified with some of the most widespread and popular ways of talking about the death of Jesus, I draw on homiletical examples that show how preachers can confront misunderstandings about the implications of the cross for Christian faith and practice.

2

From Theory to Metaphor

Rediscovering New Testament Cross Talk

The last three decades have seen a robust "turn toward the text" in homiletical theory and consequently in the preaching of many pastors, especially recent seminary graduates. A new generation of homiletical theorists emerged in the mid-1970s who insisted that, in both form and content, biblical texts comprised the indispensable point of departure for sermon construction.[1] The work of these scholars reflected the influence of literary approaches to biblical interpretation, coupled with the insights of the "New Hermeneutic" of Gerhard Ebeling and Ernst Fuchs, who argued that biblical texts function to precipitate transformative "events" in experience. Proponents of what came to be known as the "New Homiletic" suggested that the sermon is a recapitulation of the event intended not only by the text's content, but also through its form.[2] Preachers trained in the new approaches sought to engage biblical texts as vehicles of gospel transformation, whose effects happen anew in the Sunday morning sermon.

Today, three decades and more later, the high tide of the New Homiletic has settled into a series of steady ripples, and in many quarters is being supplemented or supplanted by sociocritical and other postmodern approaches; yet its influence can still be felt. Thanks to the New Homiletics's robust embrace of the biblical text as the indispensable point of departure for the sermon, both in form and content, a whole generation of preachers can be found of a Monday or Tuesday morning wrestling to discover not only what next Sunday's chosen text has to *say*, but also what it seeks to *do*, and how.

Oddly enough, it is precisely such close attention to the text that has left many a preacher stymied in the effort to grant the cross a more central place in the pulpit. The fact is, whatever it is that New Testament texts want to do in relation to the cross, one thing they apparently *do not* want to do is to lay out systematic theories of atonement. New Testament texts on the cross, as we observed in chapter 1, turn out to be occasioned by context and situation. For the most part, the reflection of New Testament writers on the cross is driven by pastoral and paraenetic, or behavior-shaping, interests and not by a concern for systematization. To achieve their aims, biblical writers deployed an array of images, often more than one in a single context, calling into play knowledge of the customs and religious sensibilities of the ancient world, especially cultic sacrifice, religious law, and an apocalyptic sense of cosmic time, to illumine Jesus' death as a redemptive event.

All of this can be frustrating for preachers who have assumed that what "counts" as responsible reflection on the saving significance of Jesus' death is atonement *theory*. They can find themselves confronted by an all-but-unbridgeable gap between the form and aims of theological reflection on the cross so energetically debated in their seminary classrooms and the pastoral, imagistic cross talk of the New Testament.

Yet, what preachers experience as a frustrating gap when they open the New Testament, I would argue, *is precisely the homiletical point.* What if the local, apparently ad hoc, and sapiential character of New Testament cross talk, in all its metaphorical diversity, is not an obstacle to be avoided in preaching, but a path to be followed? Something along these lines is suggested by Gail R. O'Day:

> I want preachers to think about the Bible not as a source to be mined for its content, but as a model that can provide both warrants and metaphors for what preachers do. *If we turn to the Bible as a model for preaching and not simply as a source, we will find ways to reinvigorate our preaching with the primary language of faith.*[3]

With O'Day, I suggest that New Testament cross talk is an indispensable model for contemporary preaching, particularly as preachers today search for fresh, relevant language for speaking of the cross.

"What cries out for redemption," observes David Kelsey, "is the world as such, the embracing creaturely context in which human beings live."[4] He goes on to say that "the range of ways that people may do evil and the range of situations in which they may undergo evil is open-ended."[5] Talk of redemption, then, will have a case-by-case particularity.

Every week, preachers face specific human beings whose anguished question is whether and how God is redemptively engaged with the real situations of their lives. It is to just such specific outcries for redemption arising from the lives of particular people in particular places that New Testament cross talk is addressed. Talk about the cross in the New Testament is not abstract and general; it is pastoral speech, local and specific, crafted to interpret the saving significance of Jesus' death for a time and a place.

To achieve these ends, New Testament writers deploy an array of metaphors, sometimes more than one in a single context. Metaphors function differently and have different aims and capacities than atonement theories. No metaphor was meant to "explain" the efficacy of the cross in an exhaustive way; each metaphor could illuminate only *some* aspects of what God was doing in the death and resurrection of Jesus in relation to *some* situations. Nor did New Testament writers hesitate to combine multiple metaphors to evoke desired rhetorical effects. Deciding when and how to use particular images as metaphors for redemption was an art, not a science, and depended on the situation, setting, and pastoral purpose for which a Christian teacher wrote or preached.

NEW TESTAMENT CROSS TALK:
A SYSTEMATICS OF THE CROSS?

Although many readers of the New Testament assume that Paul, at least, takes a systematic approach to reflecting on Jesus' death, many scholars disagree. Charles Cousar, for example, cautions us against reading Paul as a systematic or dogmatic theologian.[6] While Paul's theology of the cross is not incoherent, Cousar points out, Paul engages a range of metaphors to speak of Jesus' death, choosing them with an eye not to systematic coherence or comprehensiveness, but to the pastoral needs of the contexts and problems he is addressing. The apostle aims to help his congregations imagine redemption in ways that will produce faithful practices of worship and witness.

Victor Paul Furnish is likewise persuaded that Paul "was certainly not a 'systematic theologian'" and points to "both the profoundly 'situational' character of his theology and the thoroughly theological character of his ministry." Paul's writing, says Furnish, while thoroughly theological, is first and foremost *pastoral.*[7] Paul is addressing particular contexts and situations, eager to show the difference that God's act in

Jesus Christ has made and is making in and for those pressing situations. His interpretations of the redemptive import of Jesus' death are always context-specific, vivid, and varied.

J. Christiaan Beker agrees that "Paul is not a systematic theologian, but rather an interpreter of the Gospel," whose interpretive strategy as he accommodates his message for each particular audience and purpose manifests a "dialectical interaction between coherence and contingency." In other words, to say that Paul's writing is not systematic does not mean that it is incoherent. Beker draws a careful distinction between the coherent framework of Paul's thought and notions of a conceptually systematic scheme of redemption. Within an overall framework that views the cross as the marker, or turning point, of God's inauguration of new creation, Paul employs a diversity of images suited to pastoral situation and cultural context. For Beker, the coherent center of Paul's thought is his apocalyptic worldview, in which the cross stands as the marker, or turning point, of God's inauguration of a new creation.[8] Nonetheless, his cross talk is flexible and adaptive, shaped by the contingencies of each situation and setting.[9]

New Testament writers were not primarily concerned to specify in detail the inner workings or logic of atonement. They were far more interested in *exploring the dynamics* of redemption within concrete situations that cried out for redemptive address than in *explaining the logic* of redemption.[10] Since metaphor functions so pervasively in this exploratory rhetoric of the cross, it deserves our close attention.

THE NATURE OF METAPHOR

In classical Greek rhetoric and according to the lights of a much later "scientific" age, metaphor was an "abuse of language," more misleading than helpful.[11] As empiricism came to influence theories of what counted as "knowledge," figurative language was increasingly considered imprecise and merely decorative. In theological discourse as in other discourses governed by empiricism and rationalism, *non*figural, *non*imagistic language was more valued. Systematic argumentation, with its propositional and deductive logic, came to be regarded as a more reliable means of gaining any genuine theological insight. Such language came to be regarded as more precise and therefore more appropriate for illuminating the meaning of atonement than figural language. According to British theologian Colin Gunton,

An absolute division, accordingly, came to be made between argument and rhetoric, truth and ornament, literal or metaphorical, with
all the virtues on one side, all the vices on the other. The outcome
was a belief that what cannot be translated from metaphorical into
"literal" language cannot be held to be true. On such an account,
metaphor is disqualified from being a means of our rational interaction with the world: *unless it ceases to be metaphor, it cannot tell the
truth.*[12]

It is striking, therefore, that metaphor comprises the rhetorical heart of
the cross talk found on page after page of the New Testament. Often, a
bafflingly rich welter of images and metaphors occurs in a single biblical text. Colossians 2:6–19 is a good example. Jostling one another in
this text are metaphors of circumcision, the erasing of a legal record, a
canceled debt statement, disarmed warriors, and captives led in a victory procession. No image dominates, and each qualifies all the others.
One way to deal with this apparently messy pastiche of figures and
themes is to tease the images apart, deduce the implications of each one
separately, and then seek an overarching, comprehensive, rationally
seamless explanation of the workings of divine redemption that will
account for all of them. Yet such an approach to a text like Colossians
2 risks suppressing exactly the multiform, stereoscopic diversity of perspectives on the cross that produce its semantic effect.

THEORIES OF METAPHORICAL MEANING

Aristotle, the first to try to define metaphor and discuss how metaphors
work in language, said that in a metaphor a new term is substituted for
the term we would expect.[13] Accordingly, Aristotle's explanation of
metaphor is what has come to be known as a "substitution" theory of
metaphor. Such substitution was regarded as a corruption of language,
potentially misleading and rather untrustworthy; straightforward logical statement was by far the preferred mode of expression.

The twentieth century saw an energetic revival of interest in
metaphor as a powerful strategy for generating meaning. Philosophers
of language vigorously disputed the old substitution model. Metaphor,
they said, was not a matter of simple word substitution. Instead, what
is at stake in metaphor is that a creative, semantically powerful tension
is established between two terms from disparate realms of experience.
For example, when we speak of "the sun's fury," we are employing a

metaphor that sets an object from one realm of experience (celestial bodies) into a creative relationship with a term from another realm of experience (human emotion). The tension comes from the fact that the two terms, and the two realms of experience on which they draw, do not fit naturally or easily together. Yet making a connection between the two is not completely arbitrary, either. In some sense (albeit a rather different sense) there is heat involved, and discomfort, when we experience either a hot sun or a hot temper. Thus we construct metaphors where we perceive features of similarity or resemblance between two objects or realms of experience; yet at the same time we count on the distance and difference between the two sides of the metaphor to generate fresh insight. Rhetorician and philosopher of language I. A. Richards proposed that the first term in a metaphorical construction is called the "tenor," and the second term or image drawn into relationship with the first is called the "vehicle"—terminology since adopted by many others in discussions of metaphor.[14]

Paul Ricoeur has been one of the chief architects of metaphor theory in the twentieth century. Ricoeur argued that thinking of a metaphor as a matter of substitution that occurs at the level of words is far too simple and altogether misses the heart of metaphor's semantic (meaning-generating) power. In fact, metaphor is a "semantic impertinence," something that both grabs our imagination and challenges our categories. This "impertinence" of meaning is achieved when we set an object or experience from one realm within a frame of meaning appropriated from a different realm of experience.[15] Thus metaphor is an innovation, "a semantic event that takes place at the point where several semantic fields intersect."[16]

Ricoeur identifies how the tension at the heart of metaphor generates meaning. In a metaphor, an irresolvable tension is produced by the jostling between the similarities and dissimilarities between tenor and vehicle. This tension, says Ricoeur, is creative; in fact, it is precisely what makes the metaphor "work." Drawing on the work of I. A. Richards and Max Black, Ricoeur invites us to imagine this tension as the simultaneous assertion of "is" and "is not." In other words, *this* (tenor) "IS" *that* (vehicle), but—no, come to think of it—*this* (tenor) definitely "IS NOT" *that* (vehicle). "The sun" is indeed "furious," but no—the sun definitely *is not* furious; after all, it is inanimate and cannot bear animosity toward anyone. And yet when we speak of the sun's fury, resisting either overliteralizing the metaphor (which results in absurdity) or denying the possibility of the metaphor (which breaks it apart and renders it

empty), the juxtaposition of the notion of a wrathful being and a blaz-
ing celestial body both evokes and enlarges our experience of working
under the relentless afternoon heat of a cloudless summer day. The
metaphor "works" for us as long as, and only as long as, we resist collapsing the tension that connects the two terms of the metaphor either
into the "is" (literalizing) or "is not" (denying) side of the relationship,
either equating or separating celestial body and human emotion.

When we recognize metaphor as a semantic impertinence and innovation, it becomes clear that metaphors do more than "redescribe"
something. The semantic work they do is not ancillary to meaning; it is
essential. Metaphors, in other words, are not just a decorative or more
appealing way of saying something we could have said more clearly some
other way. They are semantically inventive, creative, and disclosive,
uncovering what is genuinely new. A metaphor opens to us new paths
of discovery we could not have accessed *except* by means of metaphor.[17]

METAPHOR IN THEOLOGICAL DISCOURSE

Metaphor is especially helpful in exploring divine presence and activity
since it fundamentally aims to bring to expression a less-familiar realm of
experience by drawing it into relationship with the concepts and images
of more familiar ones. Noting that the Bible seems positively to thrive on
metaphor and image, theologians have vigorously explored the way that
metaphors work to produce theological meaning. In fact, to express in language the saving significance of Jesus' death, metaphor is neither incidental nor merely ornamental to the task, but fundamental and essential.
Why is this the case? Thelma Mcgill-Cobbler puts it succinctly:

> The very word *cross* in ancient times evoked strong emotions because
> it was symbolic of the ultimate penalty and the most excruciating
> form of death. . . . It is in light of the horror of crucifixion most of
> all that we can discern the sense in which our theological reflection
> on atonement can be said to be metaphorical. That that death by cru-
> cifixion of a Galilean carpenter was called an atoning death—
> whether as sacrifice, victory, or dying for others—could only be seen
> as an utterly alien reference.[18]

Speaking of the execution of a Jewish itinerant teacher in the first century as a redemptive action of God is, from the outset, a "semantic impertinence," says Megill-Cobbler.[19] There is something inherently and

irreducibly metaphorical about Christians' declaration that the execution of a man on a Roman cross is an act of divine redemption. Not surprisingly, then, Christians found it necessary from the beginning to appeal to metaphor in order to bear fitting witness to this confluence of horrific historical event and divine redemptive action. They drew on cultic, familial, legal, and military frames of reference, among others, to express what they experienced as God's redemptive engagement with the created order, including human experience, in the death of Jesus of Nazareth.

The fact that New Testament writers, as well as theologians for many centuries afterward, employed metaphor to speak of the saving significance of Jesus' death is not a slip or an accident, argues Colin Gunton. Each metaphor employed to illuminate the divine redemptive action hidden within the death of Jesus of Nazareth tells us something new. Drawing on scientific studies of the function of metaphors and models, Gunton reminds us that metaphors of atonement are not merely descriptive. Just as metaphors and models shape and guide a lab researcher's approach to natural phenomena, so metaphors of atonement orient us and permit "epistemic access" to the hidden divine action in Jesus' death.[20] We cannot suppose that any of our metaphors of atonement perfectly fit the situation they seek to disclose; but each contributes something indispensable to our understanding of what is at stake. The various atonement metaphors of the biblical witness, Gunton argues, bring to light different dimensions of the dynamic relationality of human beings with God in atonement—first of all in the cross, but also in our ongoing experience of the dynamics of redemption.

Metaphors in theology, like metaphors in science, are heuristic, which means that they open a path to discovery and knowledge. We seek by means of the "is/is not" language of metaphor to discover what "is"— that which Jesus' life, death, and resurrection accomplishes in human experience. Metaphors of redemption are exploratory devices that allow us to learn more about the nature and consequences of God's redemptive activity.[21]

In redemption metaphors, as with all metaphors, the "is and is not" tension at the heart of metaphor needs to be kept firmly in mind. When we speak of Jesus' death as debt payment, we do so knowing that Jesus' death both *is and is not* debt payment. We speak of Jesus' life, death, and resurrection as a divine liberation of captives, knowing that it *is and is not* the liberation of captives in a literal sense—there is no military raid on a prison camp to free one's comrades. We speak of Jesus' death as "sacrifice," knowing that the event *does and does not* fit the rubrics of sacrifice. (For example, in the death of Jesus, the human beings who "offer" the victim do not regard it as a sacrificial act; and the natural flesh of the sacrificial victim is never literally consumed, as generations of eucharistic theologians have been at pains to explain.)[22] Furthermore, the various metaphors used to disclose God's redemptive engagement with us at the cross balance and qualify one another. As Gunton and others insist, the multiplicity of metaphors in the biblical witness and in the centuries since is to be embraced, not regarded as a problem to be solved. Attempts to flatten the many metaphors of the tradition into a seamlessly "rational" explanation of redemption can only result in semantic and theological loss.

J. Wentzel van Huyssteen stresses that metaphors do not merely *redescribe* our experience; they actually *extend or stretch* the boundaries of our knowing. In other words, they are epistemically productive; and what they disclose cannot be reduced to propositional language of a more "straightforward," literal kind. Metaphor, says van Huyssteen, "is in fact a mode of speech in which language itself is stretched, as it were, to gain new insight, to understand something which was previously incomprehensible."[23] By reframing the lesser-known in terms of the known, a metaphor mines the tension between "is" and "is not" in a way that generates new possibilities, yet with a modesty that does not aim at comprehensiveness or control. Such an understanding of metaphor points to the possibility that metaphors actually function to disclose that which we could not perceive *without* metaphor: "The metaphorical mode of thought unlocks the reality of that which is referred to in religious language in a constructive manner that—true to the nature of metaphor— imparts new knowledge (*it is . . .*) while at the same time protecting and preserving the mystery (*it is not . . .*)." In other words, for van Huyssteen, metaphor is not merely descriptive but constructive; it is "creatively determinative" of the possible range of thought and experience.[24]

Of course, a theological metaphor, as any metaphor, can become "dead" when it becomes a linguistic commonplace. Familiarity has a way of domesticating metaphors, so that their original power to evoke new insight is diminished. When a metaphor becomes so commonplace that it no longer elicits an "aha!" says Sallie McFague, the metaphor loses "its recognition possibilities (its 'is' quality), for the metaphor is no longer 'heard'; it is taken to be a definition, not a likely account."[25] If I speak of the "inexorable march of time," for instance, others will likely know what I have in mind, but the expression will elicit a yawn, at best. Certain theological metaphors have become so common that their fundamental nature *as* metaphors, as opposed to literal claims, has been all but forgotten. A good example, notes McFague, is "God is Father."[26] Forgetting that this *is*, in fact, fundamentally a metaphor can lead us to underestimate both its possibilities and its limits. Overliteralize the metaphor, forgetting the creative tension—the "is not"—that separates the two terms, and everything that human fathers are and do is ascribed to God. More dangerously, attributes of God are ascribed to earthly fathers—omnipotence, for example. God is not *literally* a father, producing human beings by procreation or carrying them on "his" back. We cannot equate the *full range* of what earthly fathers do and intend with the actions and intentions of God. Yet to deny the metaphor "God is Father" *any* disclosive potential whatever is to lean too far the other way, overemphasizing (instead of underestimating) the "is not." Then we risk losing genuinely meaningful disclosures about divine-human relationship to which many Christians have long testified, and to which Jesus himself gave credence.

HOW DID WE MOVE FROM METAPHORS OF REDEMPTION TO THEORIES OF ATONEMENT?

Metaphor has functioned indispensably in the primary speech of Christian witness to the significance of the cross. Not surprisingly, though, reflection on this primary speech has led to a secondary level of discourse, the level of critical theological reflection. One way Christian thinkers have sought to further explore the implications of God's saving work has been to expand particularly compelling metaphors of redemption into more elaborate "models" and then into theories.

A model in theology, says McFague, is "a dominant metaphor, a metaphor with staying power." Theological models, like models in scientific investigation, are heuristic, testable "maps" of a field in which we are interested. They give us a way to explore further the matter at hand and provide access to the less-known in terms of the more familiar. However, as McFague points out, insofar as models represent "a further step along the route from metaphorical to conceptual language, they can be dangerous."[27] The danger is that metaphors become "solidified" and elaborated into models that can too easily be taken as *literal* accounts of the less-familiar field of interest, or state of affairs. For example, we can speak of divine atonement in terms of settling a debt; but if this metaphor is overly extended, then the entire field of divine-human relating can be inadvertently viewed as an elaborate system of commercial exchange, and all kinds of erroneous conclusions can be drawn. The problem intensifies if one model becomes so dominant that the corrective that other metaphors and models might contribute to it is lost. McFague warns,

> [Models] are necessary . . . for they give us something to think about when we do not know what to think, a way of talking when we do not know how to talk. But they are also dangerous, for they exclude other ways of thinking and talking, and in so doing they can easily become literalized, that is, identified as *the* one and only way of understanding a subject. The danger is more prevalent with models than with metaphors because models have a wider range and are more permanent; they tend to object to competition in ways that metaphors do not.[28]

As if this were not enough, under the influence of Enlightenment canons of rationality, models began to be elaborated into extensive, rationalistic theories. Sometimes models and theories favored by a particular and dominant cultural milieu eliminated competitors. As these theories took hold, they began, in turn, to structure the way Christians read the primary Christian testimony to the significance of the cross found in the Bible, ultimately tending to obscure the multiplicity of metaphors actually found there.

Charles Cousar warns that several problems can develop when the New Testament is read through preset, theoretical lenses. First, one can miss the simple fact that biblical metaphors *are* metaphors. When this happens, says Cousar, "religious literature is read with a positivistic scientism, and for that reason the theories, as interpretations of the biblical text, are often taken as exact descriptions of what God 'had to do' in order to save a lost world."[29] Modern readers (preachers included), influenced by theology's legacy of valuing the conceptually precise over the poetic, can all too easily forget that metaphors of atonement, like the taking of captives or the cancellation of debt, are meant to be poetic, tensive, evocative expressions of the dynamics of divine-human relationality in Jesus' death and resurrection, not literal conceptual maps of the "mechanics" of redemption.

A second pitfall, Cousar points out, is reductionism. A reductive reading of New Testament texts occurs, warns Cousar, when a single metaphor is extracted from among others and assigned a dominant role, in effect flattening the semantic potential of other images in its

immediate context. Cousar calls our attention to the fact that 2
Corinthians 5:14–6:2, for example, calls into play an array of rich
metaphors drawn from participatory, judicial, sacrificial, and social
experience, metaphors that together evoke a lively semantic interplay.
Yet, in a misguided quest for "logical precision," one image—commonly, justification—is sometimes taken to be the "key" to all the rest.
"Unfortunately," says Cousar, "when justification is determined to be
the dominant category and the key to coherence in soteriology, then
the other categories are likely to be constricted to make them cohere."
He is adamant that "the interplay of the differing metaphors . . . simply must not be sacrificed for 'the idea' or for a precise theory, which
in itself is orderly and intelligible but not really 'big' enough to encom-
pass the less orderly but expressive categories of the text."[30]

In context after context, New Testament language about God's saving action in the life, death, and resurrection of Jesus is richly multiform. The writers of these texts used multiple metaphors deliberately;
no single metaphor was considered sufficient to disclose all that was
at stake, redemptively, in the death of Jesus. Each metaphor discloses
some aspect of the changes in human-divine relationality brought
about by Jesus' life, death, and resurrection. Yet any one of them "can
claim only an indirect purchase on reality, bringing to expression
some, but not all, aspects and relationships" of the matter at hand.[31]
Trying to domesticate multiple metaphors of redemption within the
confines of a single unified theory, advises Cousar, "constricts their
expressiveness in an effort to make one category the interpretive key
to the others."[32]

Since New Testament writers did not deem it fitting or necessary to
collapse their diverse imagery into a single, coherent system, we should
at the very least pause before trying to smooth the texture of a passage
into a seamlessly coherent whole. Instead of compressing or distorting
most of the metaphors in a text to fit the requirements of a favored
model or theory, preachers need to let *every* metaphor in a context contribute to the text's meaning.

UNDERSTANDING NEW TESTAMENT
METAPHORS OF REDEMPTION

Four guidelines can help the preacher grasp the texture of the metaphors
found in the New Testament.[33]

1. First, it is crucial to pay attention to the way a metaphor functions in its cultural and pastoral context. Metaphors do not "mean" all by themselves—in the New Testament or anywhere else. They produce meaning as (and because) they are deployed in relationship to specific contexts, where specific presenting problems exist. We must keep in mind the overall pastoral objectives toward which the writer seems to be aiming in any context to see what a metaphor is meant to disclose.

2. We need to guard against overextending and literalizing any metaphor. Anselm, we remember, was unhappy with the overextension of the metaphor of deliverance of captives, for he believed it led to untenable ideas about God. In one widely popular elaboration of the ransom-of-captives metaphor, for example, Satan was said to hold humanity in his clutches by right because of humanity's sin. God sent Jesus, cleverly disguised as a human being, as "bait" to fool Satan. Dying, Jesus fell into Satan's clutches, who thought he had captured a prize; but the divine Son overcame Satan, delivering all human beings from Satan's dominion. Clearly, this elaboration of the deliverance metaphor has the unintended effect of making God look like a trickster and Jesus' incarnation like a mere ploy in a game of one-upmanship.

3. We can take care to be sure that we have really understood the meaning-system that a particular metaphor brings into view. Misconstruing the meaning-system implied by a metaphor has been a notorious problem with metaphors of sacrifice. More will be said of this in chapter 6; but for now, it is enough to say that when assumptions are made that the efficacy of sacrifice turns on the idea of substituting one death for another, both the meanings of sacrifice and of the cross are distorted. Understandings of sacrifice in the Old Testament (on which New Testament writers depend) are wide-ranging, and on the whole have far more to do with the gift of life than with a substitute "death penalty."

4. We can make sure metaphors are allowed to speak in their own right, without being accommodated to our favored theories, or forced, along with other metaphors, into a single, seamlessly rational system of meaning. Consider, for example, 2 Corinthians 5:14–21, a text where multiple metaphors function side by side. Here we find allusions to the death of Jesus—as a representative death on behalf of many, as an event of apocalyptic re-creation, as debt-canceling, as peacemaking, and as sin-bearing for others—occur in close proximity. It is tempting to make sense of this text by adjusting all of its metaphors of the cross into one intricate system. It is more crucial and fruitful, though, to keep the pastoral aim of the text in mind.

Paul is facing a problem: the Corinthians are expressing increasing disregard for him as other, more-impressive teachers come along in his wake. So he challenges the Corinthians to see him—Paul—in terms of his cross-conferred identity, using one metaphor after another to press the point: (1) Paul does not live for himself, because Jesus has died representatively for him, and now Paul lives for Christ (vv. 14–15). (2) Paul should not be evaluated from a merely human point of view, because a new creation has taken hold in the death and rising of Christ, and all the old standards of evaluation have been rendered null and void (vv. 16–17). (3) Regarding Paul as either an embarrassment or the rival of other teachers is moot, since Paul comes only as the ambassador of another, the God who has become reconciled to us in Christ (vv. 17–20). (4) Paul's humble and altogether unimpressive self-presentation is not an impediment to believing his message; it simply stands as further evidence for the message itself, that our worth lies in the fact of the great exchange accomplished in Jesus' death, in which Christ became as we are that we might become as he is—that is, set right with God (righteous, v. 21), regardless of human estimates of our worth. Here Paul's aim is to employ multiple metaphors of the cross to press home a point with the Corinthians—that his unremarkable demeanor is appropriate to cross-shaped existence. Paul shifts the debate about his authority to new, cross-established ground. His aim is not to construct a single grand soteriological system.

A related problem is for the biblical interpreter to read every metaphor of redemption through his or her own, preset scheme of thought. For example, some interpreters have unwittingly fallen into the habit of reading every text through penal substitutionary lenses when that view is completely absent from the text or its context. Such a reading strategy clouds the distinctive function of the metaphors a writer may have chosen and impose on the text's pastoral situation concerns that were not in the writer's view.

CRITICALLY ASSESSING THE EFFECT
OF THE METAPHORS WE USE

Metaphors, no less than theories, need to be subjected to critical reflection when used in contemporary contexts. "What do we do," Renita

Weems asks, "when metaphorical language ends up creating more problems than it solves?" Rightly noting that "metaphors cannot be separated
from the sociohistorical contexts that generate them and the sociohistorical contexts to which they seek to respond," Weems argues that biblical
metaphors need to be examined for continued relevance in light of their
interaction with a changing social context.[34] This is especially relevant
when it comes to atonement metaphors, both in terms of the sociohistorical contexts and assumptions out of which they have been generated
and their semantic import in concrete, ever-changing situations.

Theologian Peter Schmiechen has proposed a four-dimensional
strategy for analyzing the claims and implications of atonement theories, a strategy that I find equally helpful for exploring the implications
of a metaphor. Schmiechen suggests that every atonement theory either
specifies or implies: (1) a characterization of God's opposition to sin,
evil, and whatever diminishes the creation, including human well-
being; (2) an account of how and why God is intent on addressing these
destructive forces; (3) a vision of what it looks like for humanity and
creation to be "redeemed"; and (4) a way of envisioning the dynamic of
redemption—what God does to effect creation's redemption (specifically, in the Christian view, by way of Jesus' death on the cross).[35]

Metaphors of redemption do not work with the same comprehensiveness or precision as theories. Yet four parallel dimensions of analysis
suggest themselves:

1. A metaphor of redemption tends to bring into view a particular
   way of characterizing the *human predicament,* and, by implication,
   God's opposition to that which diminishes human well-being. For
   example, consider the ransom metaphor (liberation from
   bondage). Here the human predicament is envisioned as the captivity of human beings to sin, to their own passions, or to systems
   and powers that hold sway over them.
2. The metaphor suggests *something of the nature of God,* since it
   characterizes God as opposed to the kind of predicament in number 1 above. Unlike atonement theories, metaphors do not seek
   to "explain," and therefore, unlike atonement theories, they do
   not try to tell us "why" God confronts destructive forces. They
   are heuristic, however, opening up our understanding of God's
   orientation to the human predicament. The ransom metaphor
   helps us understand that God is opposed to every form of human
   bondage and is committed to our freedom at every level of
   human experience.

3. The image projects, within a range partly determined by the contexts with which it interacts, a *vision of what it looks like to be redeemed.* For example, when oppressive powers no longer hold sway over them, captives begin to experience self-determination and freedom of action. The ransom metaphor becomes an imaginative lens that can help us discover what liberation from bondage will look like in specific contexts.

4. The image implies a particular *dynamic of redemption.* In other words*, something is done* that alters the condition of human beings (or of all creation), delivering them from the predicament envisioned in number 1, moving them toward the being-redeemed state (no. 3). The metaphor of liberation implies that at the cross, Jesus grapples with and defeats enslaving powers.

With this four-way analysis in hand, we can ask how a given metaphor lines up with the concrete experience of the persons we hope to address. The ransom metaphor functions differently for relatively comfortable Christians with considerable powers of self-determination than for a community of Christians in Central America at the mercy of local landlords; in many contexts, it may function differently for women than for men. Not all metaphors of redemption will function equally well even for those in a single congregation, and this suggests the importance of using many different images to interpret the saving significance of the cross.

DISCERNING REDEMPTION IDEAS IN THE CONGREGATION

Congregations, or multiple groups within them, entertain some working understandings of redemption that, in more-or-less clear ways, include the same four elements we have just discussed. Through pastoral conversation, experience, and other observations, a pastor can usually discover the reigning assumptions in the congregation about: (1) what it is in their experience that cries out for redemption (sin, suffering, injustice, and so on); (2) assumptions about God's disposition toward humanity (motivated by love? wrath?); (3) a vision of what it looks like to be redeemed (being guilt free, liberated, made whole, reconciled); and (4) a sense of what God does to redeem (gives, forgives, liberates, empowers). Multiple "imaginations" of redemption may be in play—sometimes harmoniously, sometimes working in tension with one another.

Our preaching about the saving significance of Jesus' death will be more effective if we take these dominant congregational understandings into account. A majority of the congregation, if asked why they believe we need God's redemptive intervention in Jesus Christ, might answer that "we need as individuals to be saved from our sins." However, conversations overheard at board meetings and committee meetings, in coffee hour and in the parking lot, may tell a different story, revealing, for example, that this congregation needs to be delivered from fearful resentment of new groups moving into the neighborhood, persons that congregation members do not trust or like, those with whom they do not identify: in short, persons who are "Other."

The pastor who listens carefully to informal conversation, pastoral situations, and extemporaneous prayers will pick up the assumptions or implicit questions congregants have about God and God's disposition toward human beings: Is God's redemptive action in Jesus motivated by God's anger at sin, or by God's love for humanity? Should we understand that God "punished" Jesus for our sins? Is God fundamentally forgiving? Is God seen as liberator, friend, parent (loving, or perhaps and sadly, abusive)? God-images can be the source of deep, pervasive, and lasting pain in people's lives, or the source of sustained, life-giving, love and generosity.

There is no substitute for paying attention to the specific questions that immediate congregational situations and experiences precipitate—particularly if they evoke questions that widely shared congregational views of redemption do not seem adequately to answer. The personal, community-wide, or global situations that compel us and our congregations to ask new questions about the meaning of God's saving initiatives toward us and toward creation are wide-open opportunities to risk exploring the saving significance of Jesus' death in our preaching. If a congregation's understanding of the scope of redemption is narrow, this can be disastrous when tragedy strikes the community. If a congregation's dominant vision of redemption has to do with sin, guilt, and punishment, then there can be a tendency for suffering to be understood as a moral lesson. Sufferers in the church— for example, someone diagnosed with chronic or life-threatening disease, or the family of a child tragically killed on the highway—may be told by church members that God is "teaching them something." Preachers need to broaden their congregations' redemptive imagination if for no other reason than as much as possible to prevent situations such as these.

GUIDELINES FOR CONTEMPORARY PREACHING

This exploration of the rhetorical form and pastoral aims of New Testament cross talk yields four guidelines that can guide preachers in constructing sermons on the death of Jesus that "imagine" redemption in ways that connect with the congregation:

1. To speak about redemption, we can construct sermons that rely on *metaphor rather than theory.* Constructing a single, comprehensive, systematic account of the *logic* of redemption for all situations and cases is not the preacher's task. The preacher's cross talk is more like the metaphorical cross talk of the New Testament than the language of the systematicians. Since metaphorical meaning is open, tensive, and evocative, it resists such semantic "closure." At the core of a metaphorical expression is the "is-and-is-not" that arises from the perceived similarity, yet irreducible difference, between the two terms (and two realms of meaning) drawn together by tenor and vehicle. Jesus' death is and is not a sacrifice, is and is not an act of emancipation of captives, is and is not debt payment. Closure of meaning would mean that we insist on a *literal* identity between Jesus' death and sacrifice or debt payment or a military maneuver on behalf of prisoners—as if to understand sacrifice or debt payment or a military liberating action would be to understand fully, completely, and without remainder everything that Jesus' death is and does. By contrast, a pastoral, metaphorical rhetoric of redemption will be more *exploratory* than *explanatory,* as well as tensive, open, and modest.

2. As they embrace the metaphorical character of atonement language, preachers will find themselves *making a fundamental shift from "explanation" to "exploration"* **in their understanding of their preaching task.** As we have noted, theologian David Kelsey suggests that helping people grasp what God has done and is doing to redeem them in their real, daily circumstances requires the work of creative imagination instead of explanation. This is not by any means to say that our cross talk should not be "theological." It *will* be theological—but *practically* theological, aimed at disclosing the dynamics of God's redemptive activity within the daily realities of human experiences of sin and suffering, oppression and natural disaster. Imagination, Kelsey explains, does not mean make-believe, or inventing something that is not real; rather it means "to grasp the whole of something in its singular and concrete particularity."[36] To "imagine redemption" is to discover the difference that the death of Jesus makes right here and right now.

3. As preachers, we need to *connect metaphors of redemption* **with the immediate and gripping dilemmas our congregations face.** News of what God has done in Jesus Christ to redeem us in the New Testament is not a theological abstraction; it is timely good news about what God has done and is doing in relation to particular situations crying out for redemptive address. Our pulpit cross talk, like New Testament cross talk, needs to be local and located speech that traces connections between God's presence at the cross and God's ongoing, active, redemptive engagement with our lives on every level, from the intensely personal to the global.

4. *Multiple metaphors, not a single metaphor or model,* **will allow the preacher to address the good news of redemption to the multiple situations, and/or multiple constituencies, in the congregation.** The sheer multiplicity of metaphors in the New Testament, sometimes in a single context, is an invitation to risk creative, diverse cross talk in the pulpit. Preachers can deploy multiple metaphors of redemption in their sermons, turning them loose in relation to concrete human experiences to disclose the dynamics of redemption within those situations. Embracing a single metaphor and applying it in any and all situations is as limiting as single-theory interpretation. Trusting the disclosive effect of multiple metaphors, deployed on different occasions or even in a single sermon, creates space for listeners to discern the significance of the cross in relation to their experience. Different metaphors will connect for different listeners. As multiple metaphors coexist and interact, they produce flexible, lively "imagination" about God's redemptive activity among us.

Cross talk in preaching today is not—and should not be—a simplified course in atonement theory, but imaginative, pastoral speech undertaken from and for the realities of congregational life that cry out for redemptive address. This is not to say that there is not a place for theorizing about atonement in a theology-as-*scientia* mode. Atonement theories can help us think critically about the implications of claims we make in preaching. Reflecting critically on the saving significance of Jesus' death in a theology-as-*scientia* mode has its place in a preacher's interpretive work on the way to the pulpit. George Lindbeck suggests that doctrines display the "grammar" of Christian faith.[37] Schmiechen explains that "theories of atonement . . . attempt to provide an internally coherent explanation of Jesus' life, death, and resurrection."[38] It is not incidental that every theory of atonement is, in a sense, an elaboration of a particular concept or metaphor.[39] That each has been significantly shaped by the sociocultural context in which it was developed is not incidental; it should come as no surprise that these theories have proved to be more persuasive and illuminating in some contexts than in others. Yet, as helpful as atonement theories can be as we test the power and limits of the metaphors we use, they themselves do not "preach." New Testament cross talk—pastoral, open-ended, modest in its scope and aims—provides a better guide for contemporary preaching.

The varied, tensive nature of New Testament cross talk can seem to those trained in a more systematic, theory-centered approach like impediments to effective preaching. Yet these characteristics turn out to be precisely the clues preachers need to restore talk about Jesus' death to a more central place in preaching today. The pastoral and practical requirements of ministry will provide ample opportunities for creative, metaphorical cross talk. Since the range of situations that cry out for redemptive address in our congregations is open-ended, says David Kelsey, "the range of meanings of redemption is also open-ended," so that we can only bring to bear in our preaching "some meanings" of redemption, not "the" one and only meaning.[40]

What we need—and what our congregations long for, I am convinced—is a rhetoric of redemption that emphasizes exploration over explanation, maintains openness of meaning in preference to semantic closure, and aims at metaphorical modesty rather than theoretical comprehensiveness. Yet, as we concluded at the close of the first chapter, constructing fresh forms of "cross talk" that are artful and pastoral is but one side of the task of dealing with the meaning of Jesus' death today. Where the nature of God's redemptive action in the death of Jesus has been misconstrued or misunderstood, false ideas about suffering and about the nature of divine justice have found their way into the imagination and practice of Christians. These misunderstandings cannot be ignored; they need to be addressed explicitly from the pulpit. In the next chapter we turn, then, to this important task.

3

Challenging Cross Talk Gone Wrong

Taking cues from New Testament cross talk, contemporary preachers can open up new spaces for imagining redemption. Yet, we must remember that no congregation is a blank slate. Congregations are living texts—thinking, acting theological communities in which a variety of ideas about God and redemption shape worship, belief, personal piety, and witness. One would like to think that all of the ideas and constructs on which a congregation builds its theological imagination are good and helpful ones; but as many critics of traditional atonement theology warn, this is rarely if ever the case.

QUESTIONING ATONEMENT THEOLOGIES

Over the past thirty years, black, feminist, womanist, and postcolonialist theologians (in particular, Asian, African, and Hispanic scholars) have raised searching questions about how theologians and preachers have historically interpreted the saving significance of Jesus' death. Although their approaches vary, these theologians hold in common two key methodological principles. First, they do their theological work conscientiously *from* and *for* a place, stressing that all our reasoning and action is undertaken from our particular contexts and assumptions.[1] The "places" from which black, Asian, African, feminist, and womanist theologians work are concrete places marked, in particular, by economically precarious existence, social marginalization, and political oppression.

Second, these theologians are committed to doing theology with close attention to the *effects* of doctrines on the thinking and practices of believers. They remind us that we cannot really understand what a doctrine of atonement "means" without paying attention to the way it has been appropriated to shape practices in concrete contexts. They question the practical *effects* of Christian doctrine (which, many point out, has largely been produced by economically and intellectually privileged white males) when it is used in preaching and teaching among the dispossessed and those with little social power.

One need look no further than the Crusades to recognize that the cross has all too often been used to legitimate violence rather than challenge and stem it. Yet the problematic history of the cross as a symbol of military conquest is only part of the story. When Jesus' innocent suffering is portrayed as the direct result of divine design, it can appear not only to sacralize suffering, but also to legitimate the use of violence for "good" ends by those who happen to have the power to use it. To the victims of abusive power, the notion that God "willed" the death of Jesus on a Roman cross, and that this death is indispensable to divine redemption, can be deeply troubling.

Because the place from which critique and interpretation is undertaken is always specific and concrete, it is risky to generalize about the way various critical-contextual theologians have assessed atonement traditions. Yet, four common themes about atonement theory do regularly appear in the work of individual African American, postcolonialist, feminist, and womanist theologians: (1) how God is portrayed; (2) the characterization of sin; (3) connections between Jesus' sacrifice and suffering and situations of self-sacrifice and suffering today; and (4) the implication that justice is predominantly a matter of retribution and punishment. These topics are viewed as the site of especially troublesome concepts in atonement thought whose consequences reverberate across the whole web of Christian theological reflection, piety, and social practice.

The Portrayal of God

One major focus of concern about traditional atonement thought has to do with what these theories may imply about God and God's motivations in redemption. Some theories (most notably versions of penal substitution, which I discuss at more length later in this chapter) seem to make God's wrath, rather than God's love, the motivation behind the cross. If wrath is emphasized, it can seem that at the center of the redemptive drama is an angry father abusing a compliant child. In fact, charged Joanne Carlson Brown and Rebecca Parker in one of the early essays on the subject, this picture amounts to nothing short of "divine child abuse."[2] Critics do not claim that the notion of divine "wrath" against sin at every level of human relations and against its attendant destructiveness is unfitting in Christian theology. Indeed, unless we are willing to retain the idea that God is outraged by sin and evil and their effects, we cannot really claim that God is decisively committed to goodness and justice. Yet whatever their intent, some versions of penal atonement theology come dangerously close to presenting a raging, overwhelmingly powerful father figure unleashing his fury against a passive child.

One source of this distorted image of atonement is a failure to keep firmly in mind the Trinitarian context of God's saving acts. As soon as we begin to think in terms of a "divide" in the divine will, forgetting that Jesus is not a victim but fully involved in and committed to the divine confrontation with evil, beginning to end; or as soon as we imagine an inequity in power between persons of the Trinity at the cross—atonement theology goes off the rails. "A Trinity doctrine with images of mutuality and a common divine graciousness . . . renders incomprehensible the charge that atonement is divine child abuse," writes Reformed theologian Leanne Van Dyk.[3] God does not stand aloof from the suffering of Jesus as humanity's representative; God is fully involved in the suffering and death that happened on the cross. By undergoing with us in Jesus Christ the destructiveness of sin and evil, God takes into God's own self the fury of these powers, undergoing death. From this perspective, Jesus Christ is not God's victim, but is in fact God's bodily engagement with all that is destructive of human life, including sin.

Theologians disagree whether a more robust doctrine of the Trinity is sufficient to counteract the impression left by some versions of atonement theology that Jesus is God's victim. Preachers must be alert to the possibility that precisely that impression arises in popular culture—not least in Christian books, films, and music that shape the imagination of those in their pews.

The Problem of Sin

A second focus of concern among contemporary theologians is how atonement theologies characterize human sin. Every interpretation of

Jesus' death as a saving event includes assumptions about the nature of the problem that needs to be overcome, and at the center of many theories is the problem of human sin.

Critics worry that the way sin is characterized in many traditional theologies leaves out the experience of many people, particularly women and victims of unjust systems. First of all, women's sense of sin does not necessarily fit the "standard" model of sin as pride and overreaching. Instead, many women's sin consists in a failure to claim selfhood and agency. In addition, critics charge, atonement theories that focus narrowly on sin as the debt of the individual sinner before God can ignore the fact that human sin includes abuses of power that are social and systemic.

When sin is defined exclusively and for all persons as pride or willfulness, victims of abuse can feel guilty about their impulse to assert themselves and resist their victimization. Darby Kathleen Ray writes:

> For women and children in abusive situations, the definition of sin as willfulness or pride can have devastating effects as it encourages victims of abuse not to resist, not to fight back, but to remain passive and compliant, to sacrifice their own concerns and needs for another, and then to despise their powerlessness and compound the inevitable self-loathing that results from acquiescence to violence.[4]

Sin, reconsidered from the perspective of at least some women's experience, can mean *not* overweening self-assertion, but its opposite: specifically, self-abnegation and the failure to embrace and protect the God-given self. We have already noted that, on occasion, Christian pastors and well-meaning lay Christians have used precisely this logic to send abused women home to submit to their husbands' violence. Unless descriptions of Jesus' willing acceptance of suffering and death in accord with the divine will are counterbalanced by emphasis on the assertiveness of Jesus' confrontation with abusive, life-destroying powers, atonement theology deprives victims of the spiritual resources they need to resist their victimization.

Postcolonialist interpreters of Christian theology also worry about limited and limiting definitions of sin. They stress that any account of atonement must be capable of illuminating and addressing the social and systemic dimensions of sin and evil, particularly webs of influence in which ecclesiastical, economic, and political powers collude to privilege some and silence others. If sin is only pictured individually, congregations can be indifferent, failing to pursue in robust ways God's justice in a world of inequity and injustice. Visions of salvation that involve the removal of sin's "stain" or that speak only of individual debt or fault do not attend sufficiently to the commitment of God to liberate not only humanity from bondage, but also society and all creation. Atonement theologies have often been weak in showing how Jesus' whole career—his life and ministry no less than his death and resurrection—are indispensable to an adequate understanding of salvation from the grip of enslaving powers.

For Douglas John Hall, the very fact that atonement theologies focus so exclusively on the sin problem is *itself* a theological problem. Important as it is to discuss the nature of sin and evil when talking about divine reconciliation, says Hall, preoccupation with sin can leave the impression that God's motivation for redemption is creation's depravity, not creation's belovedness. If our vision of salvation loses sight of divine love, argues Hall, it needs to be revised:

> If there is a cross at the center of this faith, it is because the God who is our human source and ground cares infinitely about the creation and, especially, about that creature that is the creation's articulate center, steward, and representative.[5]

Jesus as the Model for Self-Sacrifice and Suffering

Another flash point in the atonement debates has been the relationship that some atonement theology seems to draw between Jesus' self-sacrifice and human self-sacrifice, and between the value of Jesus' suffering and of human suffering in general, regardless of cause. Speaking of Jesus' suffering as a model of patient endurance under trial and celebrating his physical pain can lend an aura of the holy to all suffering and torture. When Jesus is held up as a model of patient suffering to women and children who sit in the pews on Sunday morning covering bruises inflicted at home the previous night, the effects can be disastrous, even if unintended. They can leave worship imagining that their suffering is a privilege that helps them identify with the One who suffered on the cross, with their impulse to resist the abuser now suppressed.

James Cone has observed that atonement theology also was used to justify the institution of slavery and, by extension, colonialist oppression.[6] In areas of the world that have suffered the effects of a colonizing Christianity and where vast numbers of people remain poor and politically disempowered, Good Friday traditions with processions celebrating the suffering Christ far outstrip Easter in popularity. This veneration of the "poor man of Galilee" is a mixed legacy, argues Georges Casalis, who sees such pieties as dangerous and counterproductive for impoverished Latinos suffering under oppressive political regimes. Casalis charges that identifying with the suffering Christ encourages political passivity.[7] Reflecting on the dangers of a piety that valorizes suffering itself, D. K. Ray writes, "Redemption from evil must mean more than suffering through it together. . . . If salvation is to be a world-transforming affair, . . . then it must include *resistance* to evil, struggle against its causes, concrete efforts to undo it."[8]

Justice as Retribution

Finally, some critics argue that the favored ways of speaking of the saving significance of Jesus' death often sponsor a retributive, punitive understanding of divine justice. Homiletician L. Susan Bond observes that, as the classic *Christus Victor* image of atonement was displaced by Anselm's satisfaction theory, and this in turn was modified and elaborated in a penal direction, the effect was "a series of shifts from a Christology of reconciliation that saves the world from demonic power to a Christology of retribution that saves the world from divine wrath."[9] This shift was accompanied by a move from an understanding of justice as "making right" to justice as punishment of criminality and exacting retribution.

When the motivation for atonement is merely the payment of a debt to law, argues theologian Douglas John Hall, faith becomes

> the legal currency by which believers met their share of the debt owed to God on account of their unrighteousness. . . . Faith, in this forensic understanding of justification, constituted our appropriation of Christ's once-for-all payment of this debt, almost as if it were our becoming registered members of the bank and drawing upon this account. . . . An economy that dealt in debt and payments and loans and interests and so forth could understand this language, and if it did not in fact invent it, at least contributed greatly to its currency.[10]

Historian Timothy Gorringe contends that "what [Anselm] bequeathed to posterity was the insight that atonement and a retributivist view of punishment belong together."[11] Gorringe raises questions about the continuing close relationship between certain assumptions about criminal justice and today's dominant penal atonement accounts, asking, "Could it be that the preaching of the cross not only desensitized us to judicial violence but even lent it sanction?"[12] He argues that although a "powerful tradition" in atonement theology "reinforced retributive attitudes," an alternative tradition of justice based on reparation rather than retribution, a tradition that Gorringe finds "more squarely rooted in the founding texts," existed alongside the assumption of the necessity of retribution that underlay both criminal codes and theologies of the cross.[13]

Anabaptist theologian J. Denny Weaver sees the history of atonement theology as a theological accommodation to the assumption that violence is the necessary means of ensuring justice.[14] Satisfaction atonement theories, in particular, Weaver contends, assume "that doing justice or making right means to punish and . . . an offense is balanced by punishment equal to the offense."[15] Committed to nonviolence as fundamental to the Christian gospel, Weaver agrees with many contextual theologians that "every form of the satisfaction motif assumes divinely initiated or divinely sanctioned violence—the Father needing or willing the death of the Son as the basis for satisfying divine honor or divine justice or divine law."[16] Weaver argues that this assumption that violence is a necessary corollary of redemption cannot be easily reconciled with the picture of the nonviolent goals of God's creative and redemptive action to which the New Testament attests, and the nonviolent means by which Jesus promoted those goals in the narrative that the New Testament tells. The only sense in which Jesus' violent death was "required," Weaver contends, is that it was exacted by powers opposed to God's nonviolent form of power. Jesus pursued unswerving fidelity to God's nonviolent means of dealing with sin, even at the cost of undergoing a violent death. Darby Ray makes a similar point: "The very *process* of atonement must reflect the meaning of salvation, the particular character of redeemed existence."[17] Indeed, envisioning divine justice as retributive rather than reparative, and the violence of Jesus' death as somehow a necessary response to human sin, has a profound effect on the way we interpret redemption.[18]

PENAL SUBSTITUTION THEORY: THE NORTH AMERICAN POPULAR "NORM"

Penal substitutionary atonement theory merits special attention for three reasons. First, it is especially vulnerable to the four criticisms we have just discussed. Its portrait of God is potentially unhelpful, and its understanding of sin can be unnecessarily narrow. It may promote the idea that suffering is intrinsically redemptive and sponsor questionable notions of justice. Second, it is widely influential in North American popular Christianity. Third, although critical-contextual theologians were the first to sound alarms about the theory, it is being questioned today by many others as well.

Summarizing Penal Substitutionary Models

Penal substitutionary atonement theory can be described fairly simply (which is part of its appeal): The atonement "problem" is that (1) a holy God cannot look on sin; and (2) humanity, totally depraved, is utterly covered in sin. The penalty for sin is death. There can be no peace between God and sinful human beings unless the penalty for breaking God's laws is paid; God's holiness makes both God's wrathful response and the payment of the death penalty necessary. Jesus dies in our place, bearing all human sin and becoming the substitutionary human object of God's just wrath directed toward human sin. The saving effects of Jesus' death are applied to those who believe that Jesus paid the penalty for their sins. Those who believe are forgiven and will not suffer eternal death (the ultimate penalty of sin) but will live in heaven forever with God after they die.

Joel Green and Mark Baker observe:

> One does not need to go to a theological library to encounter the penal substitution model of the atonement. Most Christians in the West have encountered it in Sunday school classes, heard it proclaimed by pastors and evangelists, sung it in hymns and read it in tracts or books.[19]

Forms of this view, they point out, can readily be found in churches around the globe that trace their origins to the preaching and teaching of Western missionaries. Darby Ray argues, in fact, that a form of penal substitution theory, with elements of sacrifice and Anselmian satisfaction motifs thrown in, comprises what amounts to a nearly unassailable atonement orthodoxy in the West.[20]

Penal substitutionary atonement theory influences thinking about Jesus' death to a greater or lesser degree in nearly every congregation in North America, for several reasons. First, church members today seldom spend their entire lives in a single congregation as their forebears did, but tend to move from one congregation to another over their lifetimes as changing employment or new life stages and interests dictate; hence, elements of this standard account have influenced the theological genetics of a healthy percentage of members. Second, much of the preaching broadcast on radio or television alludes to and supports this standard account. Third, marketing outlets for popular, nondenominational Christian resources—including books, films, Web sites, and contemporary Christian music—largely reflect this way of understanding Jesus' death. The influence of these products on congregational imagination can hardly be overestimated. Catchphrases and slogans vouching for a penal view of Jesus' death abound on the North American landscape in every form from bumper stickers to billboards to (in my part of the United States) hand-painted signs planted in rural front yards.

Criticisms of the Penal View of Atonement

It is not difficult to see that the criticisms we have discussed in this chapter have particular pertinence to a penal view of the efficacy of Jesus' death in accomplishing human salvation. In terms of problems with its implicit image of God, Michael Northcutt of New College, Edinburgh, observes that penal atonement theory "sets the necessity of violent punishment in the heart of the being of God."[21] Divine wrath emerges more strongly than divine love as the triggering motivation for Jesus' death, for God appears to be "satisfied" only by inflicting suffering and death on a helpless (divine) child. Granted, Calvin regarded divine "anger" toward sin as an expression of God's "accommodation" to the limitations of human experience and understanding; God appropriates the range of human passions in order to interpret to human beings the status of the divine-human relationship.[22] Yet, for victims of domestic abuse, nuances like this may do little to mitigate the impression that the cross is vengeance unleashed by a wrathful parent upon a defenseless child. Keeping clearly in mind that "Christ is not a victim but a volunteer" only helps a bit; in too many homes, children have "volunteered" to become the target of a parent's fury to protect someone else in the household.[23] Holding together the single will of the persons of the Trinity in salvation can mitigate somewhat the impression that the first person of the Godhead is pitted against the second, but other problems are less easily set aside.

This model makes the redemptive efficacy of Jesus' death seem oddly disconnected from the substance of his life and ministry. Only Jesus' innocence was required if the whole point was for him to pay the price of sin. How this connects with the specifics of all that Jesus did and taught is not terribly clear. Penal substitution theory can obscure the fact that Jesus' death was the consequence of his fidelity to God's reign and his unswerving pursuit of truth-telling and acts of healing that testified to that reign. No account of the saving significance of Jesus' death can stand if it implies that it was little more than an arbitrary deal struck between two persons of the Godhead to solve the sin problem, or a horror demanded by God to balance a heavenly ledger.

One must also question whether the view of sin at the core of penal substitution theory is sufficiently broad and encompassing. Green and Baker argue that the penal view is rooted in an individualistic model of criminal justice that owes far more to Western legal culture since the Enlightenment than to the Bible. It can make atonement appear to be a legal transaction struck between the first and second persons of the Godhead (Father and Son), render the resurrection all but superfluous to redemption, and leave little room for demonstrating the significance of redemption for the shaping of Christian life.[24] If Jesus' death is necessary only to satisfy a legal requirement, and that requirement is once and for all satisfied, then it is hard to see what bearing Jesus' death has in terms of patterning Christian life or witness in any meaningful way. As we have seen in chapter 2, relegating the cross to the role of a "fix" for sin props the door open to triumphalist interpretations of the Christian life quite foreign to Jesus' repeated teachings that his disciples will share his suffering. Furthermore, thinking of sin as individual lawbreaking can obscure other ways of viewing human sin—for example, as the rending of community trust or as social collusion in the oppression of the poor or politically weak.

The assumption is frequently made that the penal substitution theory is biblical, as Steve Chalke, Baptist minister to a London congregation, observes: "Many supporters of penal substitution, following [Charles] Hodge's lead, tend to hold it as a 'God-given truth'—the only valid explanation of the atonement. . . . Thus it is not uncommon for many evangelicals to regard it as 'the' biblical view of the atonement."[25] Green and Baker agree, arguing that despite Hodge's comprehensive effort to demonstrate unequivocal biblical support for the penal substitution theory, he actually brought to his readings of biblical texts a preset theoretical bias toward penal theory and adjusted his readings to fit this view.[26] Not only is it extremely difficult to reconcile the full spectrum of New Testament metaphors with a penal view of Jesus' death, but also where metaphors of substitution occur, the notion of bearing punishment is largely absent. Peter Schmiechen likewise finds that many readers of the Bible assume that there is far greater biblical support for the penal view of Jesus' death than can actually be found there, and he concludes that despite abundant allusions to the penal substitutionary view in hymns, "it is not in the Bible."[27]

Penal theory is so widely taught and unquestioningly assumed among North American Christians that only with difficulty can many recognize that this particular account of the redemptive significance of Jesus' death does not fit many biblical texts. Moreover, a penal view, particularly if it is considered the *only* orthodox view of the significance of Jesus' death, gives us no help in understanding how God is redemptively engaged with human suffering or with the brokenness of the cosmos itself. Furthermore, penal substitution theory is among those theories that stresses the "objective" side of the efficacy of the cross but gives little insight into the continuing difference that the cross makes in the shaping of Christian living and witness. "To suggest that our debt to justice is paid," writes theologian Paul Fiddes, "certainly expresses the once-for-allness of the cross of Jesus. But it does not integrate the human response to God, and the healing of human personality here and now, into the act of atonement."[28] At best, such integration comes as an afterthought, where Christian living is expressed (paradoxically) as a kind of grateful indebtedness, although the specific ethical consequences of this grateful indebtedness are often left vague.[29]

There are able theologians today who argue that we should retain the penal model as one among an array of metaphors of atonement. Theologian Hans Boersma seeks to make this case. He does insist, as do I and many others today, that we need to be clear that our images of redemption, including the penal image, are indeed metaphors rather than literal, detailed accounts of the inner workings of redemption. "Whether we speak about the atonement in terms of imitation, of justice, or of battle," says Boersma, "we are speaking metaphorically."[30] The penal model can become useful, he argues, if we reread it (and all other metaphors) through an overarching framework of divine "hospitality." Boersma argues that, by definition, divine hospitality is only meaningful if it involves boundaries that exclude as well as include. For God to extend hospitality, whatever *undermines* God's hospitality must be excluded. In a sense, sin is inhospitality to God's ways and to those God welcomes. To maintain hospitality, then, God must punish, says Boersma, in the sense of excluding whatever subverts hospitality. In this sense, the penal metaphor has its place, alongside others.

Boersma warns us against "juridicizing" the cross. While juridical, legal, and even punishment themes have their place, we need to avoid "a form of reductionism that limits the divine-human relationship to judicial categories, and that views the cross solely in terms of laws, infractions, judicial pronouncements, forgiveness, and punishments."[31] Whether this, along with the other adjustments Boersma suggests, are sufficient to rehabilitate the penal model is open to debate. Preachers may find it difficult to get across to congregations with limited theological knowledge the subtleties of Boersma's insights about the relationship of divine hospitality and the necessity of punishment. Yet it cannot be denied that the penal model has had staying power in Christian reflection for several centuries, and Boersma opens one avenue toward fruitful exploration of its continuing relevance.

Saving Substitution

The chief problems with penal substitutionary atonement theory have to do with its assumptions about sin as transgression of a penal code and the cross as divine execution of the death penalty (operating within an exclusively retributive notion of justice). The concept of substitution, on the other hand, rightly understood, can illuminate something of God's radical self-involvement in redemption.

Theologian Kathryn Tanner suggests that we can make sense of the substitutionary aspect of the cross when we reenvision it within a radical understanding of incarnation. In Jesus, the Word made flesh, God assumes our humanity, taking as God's own the place of the radically "other," the sinful human being. Taking on flesh, God "takes our place," incorporating into God's own self everything that our humanity includes and implies, including our sinful estrangement from God. Taking and bearing this brokenness within God's very self, God bears its deadly consequences within God's own being at the cross. As God enfleshed, God taking our place, Jesus is our "substitute." Jesus is also our "substitute" in the completeness of his humanity, including his utter obedience, which becomes ours. In other words, God unites with us in our sinfulness and in our death in order that we might be joined with

God in the fullness of the life of the Three-in-One.[32] Helpful here may be an insight of Boersma's; he suggests that we need to think of Jesus more as our *representative*—one who stands *with* us and stands *for* us—rather than our *substitute*.[33]

Understanding substitution in this representative way enables us to see that Jesus' "substitutionary" or representative role in our redemption does not exempt us from ethical liability; rather, it shows us exactly the nature of our ethical obligation as those joined to God's own will and purposes. We participate in the dynamics of redemption when we, in our turn, enact a vulnerable self-donation toward the radically "other" like God's own. In finite and limited ways, we are called upon to be "like God, who loved our enmity to death."[34]

DELIVERING CAPTIVES: CHALLENGING FLAWED UNDERSTANDINGS OF REDEMPTION

It is not hard to understand why some feminist and womanist theologians despair of making any saving sense of Jesus' death. They suggest that Jesus' death was no more than the tragic martyrdom of a faithful man, and whatever we need to know about how God grapples with sin and evil, we can learn by considering the manner of Jesus' life. Yet with theologians of the cross (whose views we considered in chapter 2), I am persuaded that there is something about the very nature of God, and God's redemptive engagement with the destructive forces within and around us, that we can learn only from discerning Jesus' death as an event of divine redemption.

As we try to make sense of Jesus' death, what we do need to remember is that atonement theories are just that: theories, not holy writ. As Darby Ray reminds us, they "were formulated with the best of intentions" and "likely once functioned as appropriate and intelligible explanation of an ultimately mysterious event, [yet] in the context of today's world, their potential to inflict harm and to provide crucial ideological support for unjust attitudes, actions, and systems undermines their legitimacy and makes them incredible [as] bearers of transformative truth."[35] A guiding principle for our revitalization of cross talk today is that we must not appropriate and use a particular image in our preaching without examining its potential impact on concrete persons, including the most vulnerable persons, who will hear the sermon and have their imagination of redemption affected by that image.

Yet atonement theologies have had mixed effects. True, doctrines about the death of Jesus have functioned far too often as a warrant for relationships—political, institutional or domestic—of subjugation and domination. At the same time, though, some have found in these same doctrines a source of endurance, hope, and motivation to seek liberation from the sinful systems and evils that oppress them. As Ray puts it, the dominant atonement account has "diminished the well-being of some" but also "enabled the very survival of others."[36] For example, womanist theologian JoAnne Marie Terrell underscores that the cross has been understood by generations of African Americans and others not as the symbol of God's *sanction* of violence and suffering, but as God's *no* to violence and suffering. Both the symbols of crucifix and empty cross have something to say to us, argues Terrell: the crucifix says that God is joined to victims in suffering; the empty cross says that suffering and violence *do not* have the last word.[37]

A *complete* history of the effects of atonement doctrine yields contradictions. The same context-indifferent, universalizing tendencies that contextual theologians point to in the dominant theologies of the West can infect the margins, too. A tendency toward universalizing, sweeping judgments can crop up when contextual theologians overgeneralize from the margins. Drawing undernuanced, sweeping conclusions about what can or cannot function redemptively in Christian doctrine, even in the name of victims, can oversimplify the available data.

> The effects of any given idea are multiple, they vary over time, and they are often impossible to predict or control. . . . Feminists and others who criticize atonement orthodoxy because of its violent history of effects should not back down from our claims, but we ought to take care that in the heat of the argument we do not invalidate our position by embracing the very tactics of stereotype, reductionism, and scapegoating for which we denounce that orthodoxy, lest we, too, produce rotten fruit.[38]

Ray wisely urges us to remember that it is a mistake to characterize traditional atonement theology as either "unequivocally liberating for all people" or on the other hand unequivocally damaging.[39] Wisely, Ray urges us to remember that "theology should not have as its goal the articulation of singular interpretations and univocal truths but should aim to multiply possibilities, to open up various vistas of meaning, . . . recognizing at all times the contingent, contestable character of all our constructs."[40]

We need to resist *any* single-theory approach to atonement, however well intentioned. Several contemporary theological projects attempt to construct more usable and plausible theories of atonement, yet still tend to recommend a single-lens approach to the subject. Versions of ransom theory have proved to be persuasive to many contemporary critics of satisfaction or penal theory; but here, too, the possibility remains that we will read all New Testament texts through a single interpretive lens, accommodating the diverse metaphors of various texts to fit our preferred theory and losing sight of the deliberate diversity and metaphorical openness of New Testament cross talk, as well as the way these images interact with specific pastoral contexts and purposes.

The Preaching Task: Critical as Well as Constructive

Given these concerns, preachers face a challenge. Theologians of the cross argue persuasively that the cross needs to reclaim its vital role at the center of the entire web of Christian theological conviction and practice. Yet among them are theologians like Ray and Thompson, who insist that we must, at the same time, take seriously two realities: the *effects* of doctrine in real human experience cannot be discounted in assessing the worthiness of those doctrines, and the *effects* of certain traditional models for interpreting Jesus' death have been disastrous for some.

Reclaiming cross talk in the pulpit today cannot be a matter of simply dusting off and reiterating old formulas. Where a congregation harbors understandings of the redemptive significance of Jesus' death that imply inadequate understandings of God, sin, and justice, then preachers need to address the points of misunderstanding. Liberating a congregation's imagination from distorted ideas resulting from overextended atonement theories will require critical as well as constructive homiletical work.

The homiletical task is always undertaken in a particular context and against the backdrop of a congregation's assumptions and dynamics, which the preacher may have done little to set in motion, but which affect the way one's preaching is heard.[41] Leonora Tubbs Tisdale urges preachers to pay careful attention to this backdrop of theological imagination that exists in every congregation—a web of deeply rooted theological ideas and assumptions that operates within a congregation in both formal and informal ways and over many years. Preachers' sermons are inevitably heard against it. In preaching on

Jesus' death and its significance, it is crucial to discover, by means of careful questions and keen listening, what ideas already have a claim on a congregation's imagination.[42]

Avoiding Homiletical Myopia

Unfortunately, however, one source of faulty and distorted thinking about God, sin, suffering, and justice has been the pulpit itself. Many a well-meaning pastor has preached a sermon informed by a particular view of the efficacy of Jesus' death, often not realizing how the sermon's claims might impact some of those sitting in the pews. The effects of reading biblical texts through the preset theoretical lenses of a particular view of atonement are painfully apparent in a recently published sermon that interprets the Servant Song of Isaiah 52:13–53:12 as an explicit account of Jesus' crucifixion.[43] While the practice of reading this text christologically is, in and of itself, deeply rooted in Christian tradition, the preacher in this case presses the reading to extraordinary lengths: in the sermon he envisions God as the active agent perpetrating Jesus' torture and crucifixion.

A few paragraphs into the sermon, the congregation is invited to "make a muscle" and then to imagine the "arm of God" and what the arm of God does in the crucifixion. "The arm of the Lord is his power and might and vengeance," the preacher tells us. The arm of the Lord forms the Son (53:1–2); but at the crucifixion,

> the power of God afflicted his Son. The powerful arm of God came down in the fists of the soldiers who struck him and in the pounding of the reed they used to force the crown of thorns into his head. It was God's outstretched arms that inflicted the 39 lashes as Jesus was tied to a pillar. God's might was used to hurt his Son. . . . Jesus put his arms down and refused to fight.[44]

So unrelenting is the pursuit of penal logic in this sermon that instead of adjusting the theory to accommodate a prophetic text, the preacher challenges the wording itself and actually changes it to fit the theory. Alluding to Zechariah 12:10 which declares that "They will look on the one whom *they* have pierced," the preacher rejects the text: "There's no 'they' about it. 'He' [God] pierced the Son with the spikes that were driven into his hands and feet."[45] Not until God had seen that Jesus' "outstretched arms went limp" did God raise Jesus up.

Similarities between the horrifically abusive scene imagined here to countless survivors' accounts of the endlessly repeated pattern of parental abuse is unmistakable: the sequence begins with parental tenderness ("the arm of the Lord formed the Son"), proceeds through unspeakable torture, and then concludes with the parent "raising up" the child again.

Reading a biblical text through the preset lens of a favored atonement theory led in this sermon to alarmingly distorted understandings of (1) the nature of God, (2) the manner of divine involvement in the horrors of Jesus' death, and (3) the relationship between the first and second persons of the Trinity. When the rationality of penal atonement theory is permitted to take on a life of its own and govern the reading of the biblical text, its logical entailments pressed so far that even the biblical text has to be manipulated to fit the requirements of the theory, the scandal of the cross is twisted into a horror beyond recognition: the scandal of God's commitment to lost humanity, enduring death for our sake, is turned into the scandal of a torturing God.

Such sermons have been preached—and, tragically, may continue to be preached. Because this is true, one of the principal reasons preachers must talk about the cross in their sermons today is to counter false notions about the death of Jesus and God's role in that death, notions wittingly or unwittingly disseminated among faithful believers who come to church to hear news of a saving God. Since women historically have suffered disproportionately as victims of domestic violence and abuse, it may be no surprise that much of the preaching today that grapples with distorted interpretations of the cross is being done by women. In the final section of this chapter, I discuss three sermons by women that demonstrate how we can challenge and displace false understanding, clearing a path for ways of "imagining redemption" that are truly life-giving.

Preaching Notes: Challenging Cross Talk Gone Wrong

In a sermon titled "The Will of God," master preacher Barbara Brown Taylor grapples with the idea that "God killed Jesus." Christians must come to terms with the crucifixion, says Taylor; "according to the historical faith of the church, it happened because God wanted it to." God's silence at the cross—God's failure to step in and end the horror—only seems to underscore that God "willed" for Jesus to die.[46] The real question is not, "Did God will Jesus to die?" says Taylor, but, "What, exactly, did God will?" What God willed, Taylor suggests, was not that Jesus should die, but that Jesus should pursue utter fidelity to the ways and will of God. It was the utter fidelity of Jesus' *life* to whom and what God had called him to be and do that led to his death. It was Jesus' fidelity to the Father's way of being in the world that got him killed: his refusal to be other than what he was, his refusal to disclaim his identity and role.

Jesus could have done otherwise, Taylor points out. He could have disclaimed his identity—as in fact frightened Peter did in his threefold denial: "'I am not,' Peter said, not once but three times. So Jesus died and Peter lived. This is the difference between 'I am,' and 'I am not.' If Jesus had denied himself the way Peter did, he may have lived."[47] Jesus' death was God's will only indirectly, says Taylor—as the consequence of his faithful life. Jesus was utterly faithful, finally becoming the object of the murderous wrath of those who could not stand his unswerving witness to the will of God. "Insofar as it was the will of God that he live like that, then God's will included the possibility of his death—not as something God desired but as something God suffered."[48]

Taylor's interpretation of the manner in which God "willed" Jesus' suffering and death has three important effects for the integrity of soteriological imagination as a whole. First, she observes, such a view integrates the meaning and direction of Jesus' life and ministry with the event of his death, avoiding the notion that the sole purpose of the incarnation was for Jesus to die a bloody death. Second, such a view integrates the fidelity and eventual suffering and death of Jesus with the lives of Christian disciples. We, too, pursue fidelity to the ways of God. Third, it effectively separates two kinds of suffering, the kind that should be resisted, and the kind that results from living with integrity. It is this latter that must be endured, rather than unjust suffering that victims suffer at the hands of persons or social systems that abuse them.

In another powerful and illuminating sermon, Presbyterian preacher Laurie Ferguson challenges false understandings of the significance of Jesus' death, particularly for sufferers and abuse victims.[49] Preaching on a Palm/Passion Sunday, Ferguson aptly begins her sermon with a reference to hymns—"those definers of popular theology." In the Palm Sunday hymns, "the language is about sacrifice. Jesus is moving to be sacrificed, and the joy is interpreted as rejoicing in the salvation that comes through Jesus' death."[50] Such an interpretation of the palms and hosannas of Palm Sunday, Ferguson warns us, "takes us in a dangerous direction." She sums up the theology either implied or made explicit in many Palm Sunday hymns:

> What is communicated to us is that Jesus was a sacrifice, echoing from the Old Testament the practice of sacrificing the perfect, unblemished lamb or goat, the unfinished sacrifice of Isaac by Abraham. Jesus is the sacrificial offering, the victim who goes innocently and quietly to the slaughter. *Victim* is the defining word. Jesus submits to this horror. He endures it for our sake, but he didn't choose it.[51]

At this point in the sermon, Ferguson is clearly concerned to resist traditional connotations of sacrifice in connection with Jesus' death. Yet to break completely any connection listeners might be inclined to make between Jesus' death and sacrifice could be a difficult position to maintain, for sacrifice is the metaphor most frequently used by New Testament writers to interpret the significance of Jesus' death. Wisely, Ferguson does not leave the matter here; she returns to the theme of sacrifice, yet she is careful to challenge first the negative effect of certain doctrinal notions of sacrifice in the lives of sufferers and victims of abusive power.

In keeping with critical-contextual theologians' assessments of atonement theory, Ferguson identifies two problems that a notion of Jesus as sacrificial "victim" sets up. "The first," says Ferguson, "has to do with the image of God. We are presented with a picture of a God who demands victims, sacrifice, and death." The second problem is the alignment that is set up between Jesus' suffering and our own—regardless of the causes of our suffering: "If it was not only okay but right that Jesus should become a victim, so should we." The message to victims, says Ferguson, is clear—but clearly *non*redemptive: "When we face injustice at the hands of a person or a system or an institution, we should bow our heads, meekly expose our necks to the blade, and submit, endure."[52]

Less than two pages into this sermon, Ferguson has deftly challenged two damaging "effects" of the kind of traditional theology of the cross promoted by popular hymnody: first, that we worship the kind of God who took pleasure in Jesus' willing submission to horrific suffering as sacrificial victim; and second, that God will be pleased if we likewise take suffering meekly, regardless of its causes. Yet Ferguson does not stop at the floor-clearing stage of this sermon.

She spends the remainder of the sermon—over two-thirds of the total—developing positive interpretations of the saving significance of

Jesus' death. First, she emphasizes that Jesus did not seek death in itself, but that his death was the result of his faithful life. In other words, Jesus' goal was to live (even if it led to death) in utter fidelity to the purposes and ways of God. "He was not dragged into Jerusalem; he was not programmed like a cyborg to go on no matter what the danger."[53] Rather, "Jesus knew his work was to hold to the vision of God."[54] Having reframed Jesus' death within a vivid picture of his faithful manner of life, Ferguson can afford to retrieve the word "sacrifice," albeit subordinating it to other themes: "To be willing to be transformed, changed, sacrificed on behalf of someone else is . . . costly. . . . Jesus surrendered himself with full understanding."[55] Ferguson makes the intriguing suggestion that Jesus may have more deeply understood what sacrifice could mean for him "the night the unnamed woman broke a flask of ointment and poured it over him."[56]

Leaving the field open for multiple understandings of the way that Jesus' death may be savingly significant, Ferguson turns toward her sermon's conclusion: "However we begin to understand the Passion for our own faith, with its layers of meaning, Jesus was not a passive victim of God, or of fate, and neither are we."[57]

Ferguson's sermon illustrates a crucial first step for preachers who want to rediscover with their congregations how the cross can function positively in Christian faith and practice. She challenges a key source of misunderstanding, clearing the way for a fresh and more insightful appreciation of what Jesus' death does and does not imply. As her sermon shows, the preacher's task differs from the task of the systematic theologian. The preacher's concern is to reflect on the saving significance of Jesus' death with and for specific listeners whose lives cry out for redemptive address—in this case, those who may imagine that suffering is inherently redemptive. Having addressed these concerns, Ferguson does not *explain* the mechanics or logic of redemption, but *explores* the dimensions of divine redemptive engagement in the real lives of her listeners and shows the difference that the fidelity of Jesus' life to God's purposes makes for them.

In "Crucified God: Abuser or Redeemer?" a sermon based on 1 Corinthians 2, theologian and Episcopal priest Marilyn McCord Adams tests the relationship of God to abusive power at the cross. In a homily as remarkable for its brevity as its insight, she faces head-on deep questions about the extent to which the cross represents divinely sanctioned violence.[58] The cross is nothing but a scandal, no matter what may be our religious or political ideology, Adams points out. Certainly, crucifixion was scandalous for both ancient Epicureans (who saw it as no less repugnant than pagan myths of gods who consort with humans, have outbursts of jealousy and the like) as well as for religious Jews, who knew well that anyone who hangs on a tree is cursed according to law. Yet our sophisticated twenty-first-century sensibilities are offended as well, since the cross is a portrait of humanity abused and abusing. It offends our sensibilities, and we have trouble embracing it as the symbol of redemption. Why this violence at the heart of our faith?

The point, Adams declares, is that the violence exposed at the cross is our violence, human violence—the heart of humanity's darkness. The cross of Christ exposes our vulnerability to letting violence take us over, as well as our vulnerability to become victims of violence. The cross broadcasts the pervasiveness of human violence, whether physical and sexual violence within the home or in battle zones where in the name of clashing ideologies, human lives count for nothing, whether in Serbia or Rwanda, in Afghanistan or Iraq.[59] Yet, we cannot pretend that violence happens only elsewhere, that it is not happening here and now: "*The cross of Christ exposes the ease with which we become abusers.*"[60] Abused persons often grow up to abuse, observes Adams; and even if we are not physically harmed, "we unconsciously act out the fears and rage of our neurotic adaptations."[61]

But, Adams asks, might the real scandal be, as critics claim, that "elevating Christ crucified to a religious symbol, making the cross the centerpiece of our liturgical devotion, seems to award such scandal the Divine seal of approval?" The cross "raises the fear and superstition that God is a child-abuser; after all, did he not *make* his Son Jesus suffer? Can we not identify with Jesus in the Garden with loud cries and tears, only to submit like an adaptive child to the father's hostile will? "[62]

It is as a thoroughly Trinitarian theologian that Adams comes to terms with this issue. She insists that we must not divide the presence and will of the Triune God at the cross: "Christ crucified does not represent an extra-punitive God taking out his wrath on a handy target." Instead, says Adams, "God determined . . . to take to himself our whole human nature—a body that could be tortured, a mind that could be blown by unbearable pain . . . to identify with us in the worst that befalls us."[63] Moreover,

> God Almighty in Christ Jesus died by hanging from a tree to become ritually cursed for us, to identify himself with the whole range of

human blasphemy: not only with Hitler's and Stalin's, with drug-pushers and sweat-shop owners, with child-abusers and wife-beaters; but also with . . . those closets of rage seemingly nuclear in proportion which we unconsciously turn to self-torture.[64]

The crucified Christ absorbs violence, both violence done and violence experienced. God judges and heals abuser and abused, "relentlessly sanctifying both victim and blasphemer with his presence," declaring in his body as law-cursed, tree-hung victim that *"nothing,* no *nothing* can separate us from his love and power."[65]

These sermons by Taylor, Ferguson, and Adams demonstrate the important work that preachers can do, and need to do, to clear away misunderstandings about the cross. When false ideas about the nature of God or God's relationship to the cross's violence are cleared away, only then can more helpful, genuinely constructive ideas take root in the imagination of listeners.

4

God in Pain

Cross Talk about Suffering

One dreary late winter and early spring, my pastoral colleagues and I at a large suburban church presided over seventeen funerals in less than three months. We stumbled and slipped with our flock through cemeteries that were heartlessly grey, their dismal landscapes a patchwork of churned mud and slick, grimy ice. Two of those who died at that bleak time were children, their deaths coming at the bitter end of long illnesses that advanced on them with greedy relentlessness. The disease seemed determined to strip from both child and parents every sweet comfort of normal childhood. Momentary reprieves were followed hard by new disappointments. Several adults who died that same winter suffered similarly, while others were taken suddenly and unexpectedly, leaving shocked, aching loved ones behind.

Dozens and dozens were affected by those seventeen deaths. Many, with remarkable tenacity, drew on the resources of faith—prayer and Scripture, the Lord's Supper and the bodily presence of the Christian community. Some sensed the mercy and presence of God. But others plunged headlong into an abyss where the old affirmations rang hollow. When your child is slipping away and there is nothing you or the best doctors can do about it, the question of whether and how God is actively present ravages the mind and bruises the heart. Does the claim that God was redemptively present in the death of Jesus make any difference amid such anguish? And if so, what difference? These are the questions that preachers need to address in response to the outcry of sufferers and the

71

families and friends who suffer with them. In this chapter I seek avenues for interpreting from the pulpit God's redemptive engagement with human suffering whether on the individual or social level.

TRADITIONAL ATONEMENT THEOLOGIES AND THE PROBLEM OF SUFFERING

By and large, popular books and Internet resources that speak about salvation do not confront the question of suffering, nor do popular praise songs and hymns that celebrate the cross. They speak of God's redemptive activity almost exclusively in relation to human sin and guilt. Yet soteriology has long been concerned with the vast scope of God's redemptive engagement with *all* that degrades and diminishes human life. Redemption has to do with far more than individual salvation from sin. Any vision of soteriology which does not include God's redemptive engagement with suffering is incomplete. As ethicist Nancy J. Duff writes, "The atonement reveals God's presence with us in our sinfulness," and at the same time "the atonement reveals God's presence with us in suffering."[1]

Traditional theories of atonement that have seemed to make sense in relation to human experiences of sin and guilt have been far less successful in helping us "imagine" redemption in relation to suffering, to borrow Kelsey's phrase again. Suffering that one has done nothing to bring upon oneself and which one can do little to alleviate cries out for redemptive address. When a preacher and congregation feel duty-bound to extract the meaning of redemption strictly from atonement theories focused exclusively on sin and punishment, two things can happen: either the cross appears to be irrelevant to human suffering, or human suffering—like Jesus' suffering on the cross—seems somehow to be a necessary corollary to some inscrutable divine plan. Far from having any sense of being held in the divine embrace, both sufferers and those who love them can sink into a horrifying dread that they are being made to pay for something they have done or somehow failed to do. Still worse, if the only available accounts of the significance of Jesus' death make sin the one and only problem in which God has any interest or from which God means to save us, sufferers can conclude that their suffering is of no consequence to God, or is at least not significant enough to merit divine attention. What if the God revealed at the cross is, after all, a God interested only in a sin-payment transaction and therefore aloof from human suffering?

Critics of such overly narrow interpretations of the redemptive significance of Jesus' death remind us that we can never overlook the effects of the doctrines we preach and teach on the most vulnerable among us, which includes those who suffer. Whenever we relate the cross to suffering in our preaching, it is essential to remind ourselves and our listeners that Jesus did not choose suffering as an end in itself, nor did he glorify suffering for its own sake. Jesus suffered as a result of his unswerving fidelity to God; but he always acted to alleviate suffering. This is only one of the many reasons it is so important to make sure that in our interpretations of the significance of Jesus' death, we do not separate Jesus' death from his life and ministry. Whatever we say about Jesus' death in the pulpit, it is indefensible to suggest that suffering is inherently redemptive or to leave the impression that apparently senseless suffering and pain are pleasing to God in any way.

The cross does speak to sufferers about a God who redeems—but how? When both preacher and congregation are committed to "imagining redemption" with an openness to a wide range of metaphors, they can work toward fresh interpretations of God's redemptive relationship to suffering. Metaphors of redemption, read from the concrete place of suffering, can connect the cross with human suffering in ways that comfort, heal, and bring hope amid hurt, anger, sorrow, and grief.

Cross talk about suffering needs to take into account a range of human experiences of suffering, from the pain and disfigurement of disease to the diminishment of life that comes from social and political oppression; from the breakup of a significant relationship, to suffering the loss of a loved one (even if at the end of a long life, and by natural causes), the financial hardship of being without work, or prolonged illness. At any given time, there is hardly a congregation anywhere that does not include in its prayers someone who is struggling through the harrowing experience of cancer treatment, advanced heart disease, Alzheimer's disease, and illnesses that tax the human body and spirit to its utmost. A vision of redemption must also grapple forthrightly with the suffering undergone by entire groups of persons on the basis of gender, class, race, and ethnicity. Still another form of shared human suffering is the widespread dismay, loss, and dislocation caused by acts of terror or natural disaster. A series of such events in the first years of the twenty-first century—the September 11, 2001, attacks; the massive tsunami of December 26, 2004; and Hurricane Katrina in August 2005, among others—have challenged preachers to speak of God's redemptive engagement with human suffering on a profound level.

In what follows I discuss three different metaphors which, drawn into relationship with experiences of human suffering, function to disclose the dynamics of God's commitment to our redemption. The first and second—the metaphor of friendship attested in the Gospel of John and the apocalyptic "turning of the ages" found in Pauline texts—arise from the New Testament itself. The third, the lynching tree, is developed in relation to the cross by African American theologian James Cone. Each of these metaphors provides a different point of departure for sermons that relate the cross and suffering. In relation to these metaphors, I discuss several contemporary sermons that effectively disclose God's redemptive engagement with those who suffer.

THE GOD WHO GOES TO CALAMITY'S DEPTHS:
THE BIBLICAL METAPHOR OF FRIENDSHIP

A little-explored biblical metaphor of redemption attested in the Bible is divine friendship. Biblical scholar Barbara Reid has explored the paradigm of friendship particularly as it is developed in the Gospel of John. She writes, "One direction that has liberating potential for making meaning of suffering and death is that offered by the Fourth Gospel, where Jesus is portrayed as a friend who freely chose to 'go to calamity's depths' for his friends."[2] Arguably, notes Reid, what trips the final switch and sets in motion the events leading to Jesus' death is his *deep friendship* with Mary, Martha, and Lazarus. Jesus "enters into calamity's depths" by entering into the jaws of death with Lazarus.[3] By so doing, Jesus in effect "lays down" his own life. Jesus' befriending of humanity is done at great risk: it is an exercise of power, not a merely sentimental gesture. He does not draw back when his friendship to Mary, Martha, and Lazarus becomes dangerous.[4] He also courts danger in his healing ministry, Reid points out: "When suffering can be alleviated, he does so through healing, forgiveness, and confrontation with those who oppose his purpose to bring life in abundance for all (10:10)."[5] He does so even on the Sabbath, placing deeply compassionate friendship with suffering humans beings, a demonstration of the will of God, ahead of his own safety. When the way of friendship calls for Jesus to stand with others and bear vulnerability, pain, opposition from authorities, and finally death, Jesus does so.

Different texts in John testify to divine friendship with humanity in different ways; and a preacher must take care to align these appropriately with situations of suffering. For example. In John 15:12–17 we find the famous saying of Jesus that there is no greater love than if one should lay down one's life for one's friends. Yet we must attend closely to the context of this saying. The friendship saying in John 15:13 occurs in a context rhetorically structured around a dualism between friendship with Jesus and friendship with the world. Such a dualistic worldview might be illuminating in a situation where church members are suffering as a result of opposing unjust political and social "powers." However, if the pastoral situation we are addressing has to do with individual suffering, taking up this text's dualistic rhetoric could lead to unfortunate, if unintended, consequences. Sufferers could imagine that their suffering, no matter what its cause, is somehow the "price" of friendship with Jesus. The suffering that Jesus predicts for the disciples because of his friendship with them and theirs with him is not individual suffering due to disease or pain, but the suffering that comes from fidelity to God's cause.

If the "place" from which preacher and congregation read is acute individual suffering, the story of Jesus' relationship with Mary, Martha, and Lazarus through the episode of Lazarus's illness, death, and return to life (John 11:1–53) provides fertile ground for accessing the metaphor of God's costly friendship with us. We learn that Jesus already has a deep, established relationship with Mary; John designates her as "the one who anointed the Lord with perfume and wiped his feet with her hair" (v. 2). When Mary's brother Lazarus falls gravely ill, his friends Mary and Martha send word to him—but he doesn't come to them immediately. Lazarus is already dead when Jesus is met by Martha on his way to her home. In conversations with both Martha and Mary, Jesus affirms Martha's faith in God's power to give life; yet by his own tears he no less affirms Mary's grief. Ultimately, Jesus brings Lazarus from death to life— foreshadowing his own fate. By raising Lazarus, Jesus still further alienates the religious authorities, who are already watching him closely; they are determined now to destroy him (John 11:45–53). Thus the symbol of the cross hovers as the interpretive backdrop of the entire story.

The story captures much of the doubt and hope that accompany our own experiences of profound suffering, both for the suffering individual and those significant others, friends or family, who suffer with them. Trusting in God's good intentions toward us, we pray for Jesus to come to us—yet there seems to be no immediate response, no rescue. Doubting God's good intentions toward us, feeling acutely God's absence, our cry is not unlike Martha's, particularly if the suffering and illness end in the death of one we love. "If you had been here, my brother would not have died," says Martha—and she speaks for all of us who have ever wondered why God did not intervene to avert cancer, accident, heart failure, death. "Only believe and you will see the goodness of God," says Jesus. Lazarus is called back to life—albeit, only for a time. (Glorification comes only in Jesus' Passion, although Lazarus's restoration foreshadows that.) The significant connection here with the cross, I stress, is that in John's narrative, the fidelity of Jesus in friendship with Mary, Martha, and their brother, which leads to Lazarus's being restored to life, is the critical ingredient that tips the momentum against Jesus and leads, inexorably, to his arrest, trial, and crucifixion. We have a sense, given that John's Jesus is "in charge" of his situation from beginning to end, that Jesus knows this. In other words, Jesus is pledged to life-giving friendship with us, sparing not even his own life to see it through. Jesus "goes to calamity's depths." He willingly enters into our suffering and shares our death with us.

Lazarus's being recalled to life is not an indication that God promises to resuscitate all our loved ones. Death comes for Lazarus before life. Rather, in Jesus, God expresses the utter fidelity of a friendship that "goes to calamity's depths" with us, so that even death will not have the last word. Jesus' friendship with us is a friendship that holds through death and beyond death, even if it does not necessarily mean rescue from the hour of death. This is a friendship stronger than death. The cross as the enactment of embodied divine friendship with death-marked humanity is more than a sign of empathy. In Jesus we experience the friendship of God that suffers death with us, enters into that deep river with us, and still holds us in unfailing fidelity on its far side.

A sermon drawing on this metaphor may need to begin with a critical move—making it clear that envisioning the saving significance of Jesus' death only in terms of the payment of sin's death-penalty not only fails to help sufferers discern God's redemptive engagement with their suffering, but can also render that suffering more grievous and God-forsaken. Having made that initial, ground-clearing move, the preacher can go on to work with the metaphor of friendship, first establishing how it is found in the Gospel of John as a whole, and then focusing on the text at hand. The story of Jesus' friendship with Lazarus through his illness, death, and restoration, a fidelity that marks Jesus himself for death, demonstrates that God is redemptively present to us in our suffering and in our death, and in the suffering and death of those we love. God has bodily entered the realm of suffering, sorrow, and death, going before us all.

GOD AND RADICAL SUFFERING:
THE CROSS AS THE TURNING OF THE AGES

No one can quantify another's suffering; only the sufferer knows the costliness of his or her own suffering. The anguish of the lament psalms may be as appropriate on the lips of the young adult who has suffered the breakup of an important relationship as on the lips of the woman silently suffering the sorrow of a miscarriage; as apt to someone enduring a long, painful regimen of cancer treatment as to the man who has been let go from his job or has suffered injustice. Yet at the same time, theologians have ventured to speak of types of human suffering that are qualitatively different.

New Testament scholar J. Christiaan Beker argues that we must distinguish between two different kinds of suffering. On one hand, says Beker, there is suffering that tests the sufferer severely and yet "stimulates hope."[6] Such experiences test and challenge us to the limits of emotional and physical endurance; yet they involve difficulties to which we can rise with grit and a community's support. In such situations there is at least the impulse and capacity to subject our suffering to faith's robust but hopeful interrogation and interpretation.

At the same time, however, Beker argues that there are human experiences that strip the sufferer even of the capacity for reinterpretation—suffering that "no longer stimulates hope but evaporates it."[7] Beker speaks from experience. Prisoner in a German labor camp in World War II, he lingered close to death due to severe illness, receiving little treatment or food. In the months and years following, Beker found that the suffering he had undergone exceeded his capacity to express or interpret it, despite the intellectual capacities and theological tools at his disposal. There is suffering, Beker contends, that defies the sufferer's attempts to gain any purchase toward insight. At best, victims of horrifying suffering may attempt a description and then fall into an anguished silence, knowing that they have not begun to convey the terror, the violation of body and mind, or the depth of despair they have felt and still feel.

It is to such suffering that David Kelsey addresses himself in *Imagining Redemption*, his evocative inquiry into the redemptive possibilities for extreme suffering. Kelsey introduces us to a child he calls "Sam," who is stricken with a life-threatening disease. Sam's situation is so critical that the life of the entire family is reorganized around his long hospitalization and aftercare. The long weeks of Sam's illness mark the family for life. Sam survives—but he is damaged, his brain chemistry so altered that he is mentally and emotionally unable to learn or interact socially in normal ways. Managing Sam's obstreperous behavior is so trying that he has to be taken out of school and costly special care and education sought for him. The entire family is profoundly affected. Eventually Sam's mother commits suicide, his siblings suffer in various ways, and his father's whole life is redefined and reorganized around the project of managing Sam's situation. At the time that Kelsey writes of the situation, Sam is an adult. He can manage marginal employment in a "sheltered" work situation, but his behavior is still a challenge for his psychologists and caretakers, as well as his father. The words and categories of faith that Sam's father and siblings have learned seem inadequate to their situation.

Theologian Marilyn McCord Adams speaks similarly of extreme and radical human suffering. Adams describes as "horrors" those experiences so devastating that they strip the human being of the capacity to make meaning.[8] They blast the landscape clean of all moral or spiritual landmarks, leaving one adrift and unable to navigate toward ameliorating insight or healing reconciliation.

Can the cross answer to human suffering of this kind? Radical suffering eludes all efforts to parse it by means of reason. Grappling with the suffering that Sam and his family experience, Kelsey firmly rejects three traditional avenues often employed to explain God's redemptive engagement with suffering: (1) the notion of evil as punishment, (2) the idea that suffering is a means to perfection, and —perhaps surprisingly—(3) the idea that God is with us as the "Fellow Sufferer who understands."[9] The problem with this third approach as a means to understand the redemptive presence of God amid radical suffering, says Kelsey, is that it lodges the meaning of one's suffering in the past. One must, in a sense, remain hostage to one's suffering in order to sense God's redemptive presence.

I contend that Kelsey is only partly right here: in the midst of terrible suffering, the idea that God is a fellow sufferer who understands can indeed be a lifeline. This is the import of the metaphor of divine friendship we explored above. Yet I agree with Kelsey that if the metaphor of the Divine Fellow Sufferer is the *only* interpretive resource available to those who have suffered through mind-blasting horrors, sufferers may indeed feel like prisoners of their suffering. In other words, if the *only* way to experience God's redemptive engagement with my suffering is to continually dwell on the suffering, I must forever define myself as "the one who suffered that horror," making of my suffering a permanent shrine. Is there no other sense in which God is redemptively present to those who suffer horrors?

I have been arguing throughout this book that we need *multiple* metaphors, brought into deep engagement with human experience, to disclose the dynamics of God's redemptive activity. Radical suffering cries out for imaginative resources that can not only assure us of God's empathic presence, but that also disclose that God is bringing about a future in which suffering will be no more.

Kelsey finds hope for Sam and his family in the promise of resurrection: "The apostle Paul . . . sees the resurrection as the event in which God begins to make good on the promise that God's end-time rule will break in. Jesus' resurrection is the 'firstfruits,'. . . though not the full actualization, of the eschatological new creation. . . . It promises new life out of living death."[10] Indeed, Kelsey reports, although Sam and his father have often been locked into cycles of mutual self-destructiveness due to the lasting scars left by Sam's illness, there are detectable signs of resurrection, "a slow process, nothing dramatic, not very consistent," yet "a process of real change."[11]

Certainly, the church through the ages has testified that the Crucified is the Risen Lord of our future. But is there a sense in which *the cross itself* signifies not only God's undergoing of suffering, but at the same time displays God's overcoming the power of suffering to destroy life and hope? New Testament scholar J. Louis Martyn argues that the apostle Paul makes precisely this claim. Paul, Martyn argues, aligns God's inauguration of the new creation *not* with Christ's resurrection but *with the cross*. Borrowing a phrase from Bultmann, Martyn contends that for Paul, the cross is nothing less than "the turning point of the ages." The cross marks the end of the "old aeon" and the beginning of the "new aeon" (or new creation). Precisely in the cross, God's new order of things breaks into the world and changes the way we understand everything.[12]

Paul speaks in sweeping terms of the world-revolutionizing effects of the cross in 2 Corinthians 5:16–21. Now that the old creation has been supplanted by God's new reality, "everything has become new." We see and understand everything differently now. We no longer see Jesus, the one on the cross, according to the values of the old age ("from a human point of view," v. 16). The figure on the cross looks like utter weakness; yet that is exactly what it looks like when the world-transforming power of God invades a world in thrall to self-aggrandizing forms of power. True power, life-giving power, breaking into a world like this one looks like weakness, defeat, and death. Yet that makes it no less God's "apocalypse," God's remaking of all things. Says Martyn:

> As Paul preaches the Gospel of Jesus Christ, where does he point? When one follows the line of Paul's index finger, one sees that the whole of the apocalyptic theater takes its bearings from the cross. For Paul the cross is no timeless symbol. On the contrary, the crucifixion of Jesus Christ is itself the apocalypse, after which nothing can be the same.[13]

To put this another way, the cross, which looks more like crushing defeat than triumph, is God's resounding divine "No!" to the power of horrors over human life. Where is God found amid horrors? God is found, as at the cross, *absorbing* the power of all that is death-dealing and life-denying, taking into God's self and overcoming by love all that would strip us of meaning and hope. Although God's power is hidden under the guise of weakness and death, God's power to turn all things toward newness is at work. Reconsidered in light of the cross as the "turning of the ages," we can discern that God dwells and labors amid radical, mind-numbing suffering for our redemption. God's life-renewing power is nowhere more profoundly at work than in those places of radical suffering where we may think God cannot be.

For Martyn, Paul's apocalyptic understanding of the cross is not merely one metaphor among many, but the key to Paul's entire system of thought. We need not necessarily agree with Martyn on that point to appreciate and appropriate the disclosive power of the metaphor of the cross as "apocalyptic turning point of the ages," especially in relation to profound suffering.[14] As Kelsey has suggested, in the face of the true horrors that are a part of human experience, both individually and collectively, metaphors like that of divine friendship need to be supplemented with resources that disclose God's redemptive engagement as more than solidarity. We need to know that God enters into horrendous suffering not only to share it, but also to defy the powers that defeat human life, physically, emotionally, and spiritually.

Theologian Anthony Bartlett develops a vision quite similar to Martyn's when he speaks of God's movement into the *abyss*—the furthest "depth of injustice, meanness, and horror." The abyss is intolerable, says Bartlett, except for the cross, which is God's "abyssal compassion, . . . more a verb than a noun."[15] At the cross, "everything is given an anarchic new starting point, a kind of bottomless 'future past' that presses on all known time in the manner of ultimate re-creation."[16] The very event that appears to represent the defeat of God by horrors is, in fact, horror's defeat.[17]

Nowhere is preaching about the cross more needed than in the face of terrible human suffering; and yet nowhere is the tensive, modest language of metaphor more needed, as well. The preacher's goal is emphatically not to explain suffering, or even to parse finely exactly how God's redemptive engagement with our suffering "works." Rather, the preacher points to the cross as God's active, bodily inscribed commitment to enter into our suffering and defeat it. In the face of radical suffering, wise preachers will not shout, but draw quietly alongside human anguish to testify, in little more than a whisper, to the depth of this divine commitment.

By envisioning the cross as the turning of the ages as well as the sign of divine solidarity, preachers bring into situations of radical suffering the promise that God embraces our suffering, not merely to endure it, but also to unleash transforming power within it. Preachers know, however, that it is finally only the Spirit who can sow the seeds of hope in the broken places of heart and mind among those who suffer. The preacher's job is to testify that the cross does not sanction our suffering, nor does it merely sanctify it. The cross is God's transformative engagement with suffering, the axis on which all creation turns toward redemption.

CROSS TALK AND THE SUFFERING OF THE OPPRESSED: THE LYNCHING TREE

Stories of individual suffering unfold unceasingly within the life of every congregation. Yet layered upon that running text of congregational life are larger narratives of social suffering; these, too, cry out for redemptive address.

African American Christians have sought to connect Jesus' death with their own lives, which have often been marked by marginalization and prejudice and lived against the backdrop of slavery, degradation, prejudice, exclusion, and disenfranchisement. In recent years, African American theologians have had a mixed response to the interpretation of the cross in African American sermons and hymns. In chapter 2 I have already cited debates among womanist theologians, still ongoing, about whether the cross can function as a positive, empowering symbol of redemption among black women.[18] African

American interpreters of the cross are concerned to guard against interpretations of the cross, particularly from black pulpits, that glorify suffering and, in effect, hallow resignation to one's circumstances rather than empower black Christians to challenge the systems and persons responsible for their suffering.[19] As New Testament scholar Brian Blount writes:

> The church was so desperately focused on spiritual salvation and the identification of its own struggles with the redemptive crucifixion of Christ that it either dismissed or accommodated itself and its communicants to the savageries of racist separatism and hate.[20]

The cross must be preached in such a way that it energizes black believers actively to resist the underlying causes of their suffering instead of accommodating them to racist systems in economics, politics, and education.

In a lecture delivered at Princeton Theological Seminary on November 16, 2006, titled "Strange Fruit: The Cross and the Lynching Tree," James Cone began by aligning himself with other black theologians who are concerned that black preaching of the cross has failed to provide to black Christians a kind of critical hermeneutic of the cross that addresses the suffering of peoples under the heel of systematic, social injustice.[21] Cone acknowledged womanist critiques of traditional atonement orthodoxy, but he maintained that the cross remains, and must remain, a central symbol of the faith of black Christians—precisely because they continue to experience the degrading legacy of white supremacy.

Sermons in black preaching contexts, Cone emphasized, regardless of subject, frequently find their way home to the hearts and minds of listeners by way of the cross. Black preachers often weave in the story of Calvary as the sermon crescendos to its closing peroration. Yet not every invocation of the cross, he observed, is equally helpful for the crucial disclosure of the redemption of black social suffering in North America. If the cross only serves to resign black Christians to their suffering, it does not function in a genuinely redemptive manner, and too often, said Cone, it has functioned in both black and white preaching contexts as the symbol of pain-free personal salvation, rather than the gut-wrenching mediation of a message of divine solidarity in suffering and divine opposition to the violation of the black body and soul.

Cone proposed the lynching tree as a metaphor with disturbing yet eloquent potential to fuel a critical social hermeneutic of redemption. The image of the American black man dying a torturous death upon a torchlit, blood-spattered tree at the hands of white supremacist mobs must be held side by side with the cross, he argued, if black Christians are to discern in the cross the dynamics of redemption, from and for the "place" of their historic and continuing oppression. Unless both black and white American Christians learn to read the cross through the lens of the lynching tree, and the lynching tree through the lens of the cross, argued Cone, the redemptive possibilities of the cross remain obscure to these communities, both those whose history is distilled in a black body swinging from a bloodied tree, and those whose forebears may have perpetrated such atrocities, turned a blind eye to them, or felt helpless to stop them.

PREACHING NOTES

A sermon by J. Alfred Smith Sr. based on 1 Corinthians 2:1–2, "An American Scandal: The Crisis of the Crucified," demonstrates the hermeneutic of the cross that Cone commends—the significance of the cross "read through" the lens of violence against society's most vulnerable. Wasting no time and mincing no words, Smith identifies in his fourth sentence a tendency of black preaching on the cross to sanction and sanctify the suffering of oppressed persons instead of encouraging resistance:

> Those times when a middle-class church dares preach about the cross are times of homiletical malfeasance and theological malpractice. This travesty occurs when poor people and powerless people are encouraged to carry their demeaning cross without resentment and rebellion but resignation, as did Jesus Christ: "And he never said a mumbling word." Very seldom is the cross preached to indict individuals and evil societal structures that devalue welfare mothers . . . as well as the helplessly disabled and the hopelessly addicted. The cross is sparsely preached as an expression of God's identification and solidarity with an oppressed underclass in need of redemption from the curse and stigma of welfare.[22]

Concern about welfare reform and concern for the underclass created by an inadequate welfare system take center stage in Smith's sermon as he summons his listeners to reconsider the message of the cross viewed through the lens of this issue. Calling in particular upon "courageous preachers of Calvary and the cream of the theological academy who speculate on the meaning of the atonement," Smith asks who will awaken ethical awareness among those "who crucify with the hammer and nails of greed." The cross brings before us the poor, still being "crucified," Smith proposes.

The message of the cross, Smith tells his listeners, "has been called the doctrine of justification by grace through faith alone," and what this means for Americans today, says Smith, is "that human self-glorification and self-deification are wrong."[23] The grace by which and in which the church lives dictates gracious advocacy for the powerless and poor. Reminding his listeners that "religious power and political power formed a most unholy alliance to destroy Jesus," Smith asks whether a similar alliance is arrayed today against society's most vulnerable. The church, Smith concludes, like Simon of Cyrene, needs to "pick up the burden of a nation," which means to "carry the cross of the poor while yearning for the coming of God's kingdom."[24]

Sermons are more often informed by a more traditional hermeneutics of redemption but even then can also point toward the cross as a symbol of God's ongoing redemptive pursuit of justice for the oppressed. A sermon by Morris Harrison Tynes, for example, takes as its text John 3:16 and evokes traditional understandings of the saving significance of Jesus' death as atonement for sin and guilt; yet he denies that the cross is an isolated redemptive transaction of the past:

> The cross is a bloody romance between heaven and earth! The cross is a human mirror of God's divine love! The cross is heaven's medicine for earth's chronic sickness! The cross is heaven's remedy and pardon for earth's confusion and sin! The cross is heaven's absolution for earth's guilt! The cross is heaven's joy for earth's sorrow! The cross is heaven's hope for earth's despair! The cross is heaven's triumph for earth's disaster! But the cross is not the ultimate reality! The cross is but an historical symbol of God's eternal involvement in the sins and grief of man![25]

The symbols of star and manger, cross and empty tomb, proclaims Tynes, together signify God's redemptive engagement with human experience; yet this is an ongoing reality, and not merely a work of God locked in the past. God continues to work a pervasive cure for humanity's "chronic sickness," a sickness that is social as well as personal.

Tynes, like other preachers in African American preaching traditions, refuses to limit his vision of the sickness that pervades human experience to notions of individual sin, or his vision of redemption to life after

death. Tynes's sermon shows that traditional metaphors can be useful
and powerful if handled with care. They take on new depth and disclosive power when the preacher draws them into relationship with the
forces of dehumanization in which too many of us collude, and from
which so many suffer.

Anglican priest Kenneth Leech works both critically and constructively
with the relationship between the cross and suffering in a sermon titled
"Healed by His Wounds."[26] Leech seeks to reconstruct positively the
metaphor of the cross as healing agent, but not without facing, in a
straightforward way, that problems have been engendered when preachers make glib connections between Christ's suffering on the cross and
various forms of human suffering. Glorifying Jesus' suffering for its own
sake as "sacrificial" can lead all too readily, Leech reminds his listeners,
to "a theology of self-sacrifice based on the cross" that proves especially
pernicious for women, who "have often had lives of self-sacrifice thrust
upon them." Leech grants no tolerance to such theological reinforce-
ment of "the role of victims and the spirituality of self-hatred."[27] He
cites the "twisted religion" of a woman who "lived off her exhaustion"
and drove others, including her family, away from her in the name of
self-sacrifice, as well as that of a clergyman whose self-abnegating interpretation of the cross amounted to little more than the "morbid obses-
sion of a diminished and damaged soul."[28]

Leech insists that there is, in fact, "nothing noble, nothing redemptive, about pain and suffering as such," although out of suffering that is
a "creative response to pain," wisdom can come for oneself and others.
Yet the heart of the message of the cross to sufferers, says Leech, is the
"dangerous" but saving image of the "suffering God." The cross is "God
in pain, God in distress, a suffering God"—and "only the suffering God
can help."[29] What the cross signifies, Leech tells us, is that "God bears
in his heart all wounds. So desperate and so dark is our situation that
God must enter it if it is to be transformed into a place of healing."[30]

The trajectory of the New Testament witness to the relationship
between the cross and human suffering is not the commendation of the
imitatio Christi through suffering, says Leech; instead, the New Testament bears witness to the solidarity of God, *en Christō*, with all human
suffering.[31] Lamenting what he sees as an increasing loss of compassion
in Western society, Leech bids us to see, in Christ on the cross, the
world's victims. Leech allows poets and authors such as Edith Sitwell,
Sheila Cassidy, and Rowan Williams to evoke images of the suffering

Christ in our midst in the person of the outcast and the ignored. When the cross enables us at least to begin to *see* those to whom we have habitually turned a blind eye, the cross becomes the healing of wounds—our own, and those of others.

A sermon by Barbara Brown Taylor, "The Silence of God," is a remarkable meditation on the sheer lack of divine response—or, for that matter, any clear sign at all of the presence of the One Jesus has called "Father"—at the cross. Yet this very silence becomes assurance of the validity of her congregation's experience of suffering. Taylor reminds her listeners that

> there are people who say that Good Friday means more to them than Easter does. They have nothing against the lilies, the trumpets, the lovely children. It is just that Good Friday, as awful as it is, is more recognizable to them. They know about suffering. They know about death. They know their way around this wreckage, and there is some sort of comfort in the fact that God knows it too.[32]

Wisely, Taylor allows the silence of Good Friday to stand. She does not fall prey to the temptation to "fix" it, too soon and too glibly, with hints of resurrection. It is no help whatever to sufferers when preachers hasten to "fix" Good Friday's silence with the idea (a pernicious one) that since God willed Jesus' suffering, the silence was "okay." Such a notion can be all too easily pushed to imply that if God is silent in our suffering, then our suffering, too, is something God "wants" to happen to us for our good. As anyone who has witnessed the suffering of a loved one knows, such a notion is one thing to accept for oneself but becomes repugnant as an explanation for the suffering of one's spouse or parent, partner, child, or friend. Consistent with the view supported elsewhere in her preaching, Taylor makes clear that the only sense in which God accedes to Jesus' suffering is that it is the consequence of the faithfulness of Jesus' life. Then she goes straight to the heart of the matter:

> This is what every believer must reckon with, . . . the same kind of silence that follows our own pleas to God to *do something*—protect us, rescue us, give us a way out. Good Friday is the day we receive no answer and must suffer that silence with the crucified one—wondering what it says about us, wondering what it says about God.[33]

Taylor has allowed the divine silence on Good Friday to function as the metaphorical marker that sets up a relationship of "is-and-is-not" between Jesus' suffering and our own. Without either collapsing or overplaying the qualitative differences between the cross and human suffering (which would be to veer to one side or the other of the "is" or the "is not" of the metaphorical relation), Taylor allows the silence of God to illuminate our understanding of God, of the cross, and of our own suffering.

An apocalyptic understanding of the cross as the axis on which the world turns toward new creation is evident in a sermon by Stanley Hauerwas on the sixth word from the cross: "It is finished" (John 19:30).[34] Hauerwas avoids every implication that Jesus' death is punishment, or that what is finished is the paying of a penalty. The completion in view at the cross is, paradoxically, the complete glorification and exaltation of Jesus—the perfection of his reign:

> This is, . . . as Pilate insisted, the King of the Jews. That kingship is not delayed by crucifixion; rather crucifixion is the way this king rules. Crucifixion is kingdom come. This is the great long-awaited apocalyptic moment. Here the powers of this world are forever subverted. Time is now redeemed through the raising up of Jesus on this cross. A new age has begun, the kingdom is here aborn, a new regime is inaugurated, creating a new way of life to those who worship and follow Jesus. Creation rightly describes the work done here.[35]

Hauerwas refers us to a notation found on a fifth-century calendar: "Our Lord Jesus Christ was crucified, and conceived, and the world was made."[36] On the day of Jesus' crucifixion, creation begins again. "Christ's terror is God's Word's human vulnerability. But, it is just this vulnerability, this surrender, . . . which draws out of darkness finished life."[37] What is finished is not merely the resolution of the sin-problem; what is finished is the work of creation itself. It is we, our new in-Christ life, that is "the finished," says Hauerwas. What is finished is the remaking of the world; and while "Christ's sacrifice is a gift that exceeds every debt," the truth is that "our sins have been consumed" in an act—God's complete vulnerability, even to death—that is the hallowing and making of life anew.[38]

Christian faith will ring false to those in our pews unless Christian preachers have the courage to connect the news of salvation with suffering. Preaching about the death of Jesus from and for the concrete realities of human suffering demands courage and imagination, as well as a willingness to face suffering in all its mystery, appalling randomness, and unreason. The full range of human suffering needs to be addressed over the course of a year's preaching: individual and social, that which evokes fresh interpretations of faith, as well as the radical degree of suffering described by Christiaan Beker, which seems to strip the sufferer of all capacity to make meaning or sense.

Metaphors of divine friendship, the turning of the ages on the axis of the cross, and the dying One upon the world's lynching tree—these disclose in different registers the redemptive engagement of God with human suffering. Grappling alongside their congregations with suffering of all kinds, preachers proclaim that amid sorrow and pain, whether we find ourselves among the brokenhearted or, to our shame, among the hard-hearted, God's fidelity to us is unflagging. The living One, who stands by us in sorrow and leads us toward hope, eternally bears the scars of crucifixion.

5

God's Weakness

Cross Talk for a Violent World

Viewers of Mel Gibson's film portraying Jesus' final hours, *The Passion of the Christ*, remember, if they remember nothing else, the movie's vicious, unrelenting violence. The camera forces us to watch as Jesus is tormented and tortured to death in gruesome stages. His blood spatters and spreads across the screen. One wonders whether Gibson actually believes—and wants us to believe—that Jesus' death was saving, thanks to the sheer degree of torture he endured. If Gibson is claiming that the violence and suffering Jesus endured exceeded what anyone else in history has ever undergone, that, of course, is simply not true. Jesus was merely one of hundreds of victims to die by crucifixion in his day. Comparable and yet more excessive tortures are being inflicted upon hostages and prisoners, children in murderously violent homes, and victims of violent crime around the globe at this moment.

We live—and preach—in a world rife with violence from bedroom to battlefield. More to the point, it is in relation to this overwhelming social text of violence that we Christian preachers stake claims about the redemptive significance of Jesus' undeniably violent death. At the heart of the Christian faith is a violent death: the death of Jesus by crucifixion. But Christians claim that the ultimate effects of this death are saving and good. This tension leads to an unavoidable question: Was the violence that led to that world-redeeming death good, then, too? Can violence itself therefore be morally neutral, and perhaps even positive, if it brings about good ends? We enter the pulpit as heirs to a long tradition of interpretation that testifies that Jesus' death actually tells us something indispensable about God's redemptive engagement with our world. But *what*, exactly, does that scene of violent death tell us about the nature of that engagement, or about the nature of God?

It is not possible, given the limited scope and aims of this book, to undertake a sustained and thorough examination of questions of violence and nonviolence in connection with Christian faith. Certainly, many are convinced that Christians must renounce violence.[1] It is not insignificant that soldiers who converted to Christianity in the early centuries of the church were required to renounce their military profession. The bearing of arms was, for a time at least, considered incompatible with professing discipleship to Jesus. The connections we make between the violence of Jesus' death, God's saving will toward us, and the continuing violence of human experience are crucial matters that no preacher can fail to consider.

REREADING ANSELM: IS GOD "SATISFIED" BY VIOLENCE?

One of the most commonly misunderstood interpretations of the saving efficacy of Jesus' death has been Anselm's "satisfaction" model. Often, Anselm's image of redemption as the restoration of a relationship through "satisfaction" is merged—even by able theologians—with penal theory or sacrifice ideas. While all of these metaphors—satisfaction, penal death, and sacrifice—do imply that something "objective" happens at the cross (God does something or contributes something that changes, objectively, the status of the divine-human relationship), they are not the same. In fact, if we understand the satisfaction model clearly, instead of seeming to sacralize violence, it excludes violence. Sometimes the idea of "satisfaction" has been mixed together with penal and sacrifice motifs in such a way that it can appear that what proves "satisfying" to God about the death of Jesus is the violence inflicted on Jesus. God's wrath somehow requires the "satisfaction" of violent punishment commensurate with human crimes. This appalling idea, Schmiechen and others point out, is foreign to Anselm's satisfaction model. Anselm, far from being the source of all the problems we have inherited in the atonement tradition, offers a distinctive view that, far from sacralizing violence as something "satisfying" to God, presents the Word made flesh as the one who overcomes estrangement and violence.

At the heart of Anselm's satisfaction model is not sacrifice or punishment, but rather something quite different: Jesus "satisfies," or makes up, what is lacking in human-divine relations. Key to understanding Anselm's satisfaction model is the concept of "honor." Honor in Anselm's world of medieval feudal social relations is not so much a debt owed by humanity to God as "right relation" among persons within a web of relationships. In Anselm's model, God indeed stands in the role of the "lord"; and in that sense, honor is owed to God. But the restoration of relationship is right "honoring" within *all* relationships; it can be thought of as akin to the biblical concept *shalom*, or wholeness—all creation harmoniously and rightly related to its Lord.

Jesus "satisfies," or makes whole, what is amiss in human-divine relationship not by paying off a debt with his death, but by the wholehearted devotion to God of his whole life. To be sure, this wholeheartedly devoted life *leads* to Jesus' death; but his death is not the point. Because Jesus would not allow his wholehearted, loving devotion to God and humanity to be compromised by the oppressive powers of his day, those powers rose up to destroy him.[2] As Schmiechen puts it, "death was not the object of Jesus' life, but the result of his fidelity to God."[3] However, Jesus' death is not the crux of the "satisfaction" Anselm has in mind. The Word made flesh lived representatively, on behalf of all of estranged, sinful humanity, a life of wholeness with God and humanity; it is Jesus' *obedience* that is the satisfaction-making, restorative act of healing that makes us whole.

Carefully rereading Anselm's satisfaction model against its medieval cultural and religious backdrop, Schmiechen shows that what lies at the heart of Anselm's satisfaction model of redemption is God's determination to restore humanity to its divine purpose—that humanity should love God and God's ways with free devotion, pursuing justice and beauty.[4] What is restored by Jesus' life, faithful and given over to God even at the price of his death, is a right-related pattern of mutual self-giving—the self-offering of God to humans, humans to God, and human beings to one another.

When we understand Anselmian "satisfaction" in this way, it by no means underwrites violence. Throughout his life and most significantly in his death, Jesus both exposes and absorbs the hostility that rends the created order and diverts humanity from its intended vocation of glad self-giving to God and neighbor. The satisfaction, or mending, of divine-human relations (and indeed of the whole created order) through wholehearted, costly love of God and neighbor is a powerful imaginative resource for discerning redemptive possibilities in a world where hostility festers and threatens to explode. Hostility is quenched by a Life that closes the distance between alienated parties through self-offering love; and this self-offering love operates in human relations and between God and humanity, deterred not even by the threat and fact of death at the hands of the violent.

THREE ADDITIONAL
METAPHORS THAT ADDRESS VIOLENCE

In the remainder of this chapter I examine three additional metaphors that disclose in Jesus' death God's realignment of the relationship between the cross and the exercise of power. More specifically, these metaphors disclose God's opposition to violence, undercutting any implication that at the cross, God planned and executed violence against Jesus. Each works to demonstrate how, by engaging the violence of human sin and evil at the cross, God delivered us *from* violence rather than establishing violence as an ineradicable redemptive necessity.

The first metaphor is "Christ the Reconciler," the one who embodies reconciliation between hostile parties. Distinct from Anselmian satisfaction and other related metaphors, this metaphor is attested in 1 Corinthians and Ephesians, in particular.

The second metaphor is the slaughtered Lamb. Here I rely on the work of New Testament scholar Brian Blount on the book of Revelation. Blount argues that the slaughtered Lamb of Revelation, who is victorious even as he bears the marks of apparent defeat, undercuts notions of power as domination and instead "wreaks weakness." The third metaphor is the "universal scapegoat," an image that emerges from the work of cultural anthropologist René Girard but is supported, narratively, by the New Testament (particularly the Passion story in Mark). After each discussion, I examine one or more sermons that illustrate how this metaphor might come to expression in preaching, helping congregations "imagine" the difference that Jesus' death makes within the violent world they confront daily.

Christ the Reconciler Who Overcomes Hostility

Where violence breaks out in households, on city streets, or in the blasted landscapes where religious and ethnic warfare plays out around the globe, it is typically fed by a poisonous stream of long-standing hostility. Hostility, the bacterium on which violence feeds, is itself sustained by sediments of bitter memory, kept vivid through the recital of identity-shaping narratives of entitlement and dispossession.

The image of peacemaking between hostile parties, suggests theologian Peter Schmiechen, is a distinct metaphor used in the New Testament to interpret Jesus' death on the cross.[5] This distinctive model, which Schmiechen terms "Christ the Reconciler," emerges most clearly in 1 Corinthians 1 and 2, although we can find allusions to it elsewhere, as well. In the first two chapters of 1 Corinthians, Paul characterizes the cross as the full and decisive expression of God's "wisdom," a wisdom that contrasts sharply with the "wisdom of this age [and] of the rulers of this age" (1 Cor. 2:6).

The cross, God's wisdom, looks like folly and weakness when measured by the standards of worldly wisdom and power, but this "folly" and "weakness" of God "shames" the wise and the strong of this world. What this means specifically, says Schmiechen, is that at the cross, God is pronouncing judgment upon the world's insistent pursuit of "claims" based on limited and self-oriented forms of so-called wisdom. According to the wisdom of the world, power is making and pressing one's personal claims, or those of one's clan or interest group. An endless clash of rival claims, Schmiechen suggests, underlies the unrelenting violence of the world: "Human beings invariably are divided by claims to moral, intellectual, and spiritual power. These claims become the basis for social conflict and violent warfare."[6]

Jesus, however, presses no claims of his own; he represents only God's claims on human life. Because he refuses to play the claim-staking game of worldly power and worldly wisdom, Jesus is nailed to a cross. Strikingly, it is precisely "those seeking to preserve religious and political traditions" who reject Jesus, Schmiechen points out. In other words, groups bent on forcing upon all others the claims of a specific, self-preserving ideology, who are willing to back up their claims by force. In the crucified One, God undercuts all worldly claims. At the cross, says Schmiechen, God "is denouncing every act of claiming as a form of violence (crucifixion) against one's brother or sister."[7]

But the cross does more than symbolize a clash of worldviews; it creates that new community in which "Christians live without claims," and it grants this new possibility to the church through the Spirit as sheer gift of grace. The power to live beyond claim-making "becomes the basis for a new way of acting contrary to the divisive claims and self-centeredness of the world."[8]

The model of Christ the Reconciler also resonates with the language of Ephesians 2:11–18. In these verses, no less than four metaphors envision how the cross reveals God's redemptive overcoming of the hostility of rival, claim-making parties. At the cross, says the writer, (1) those who were aliens to the community of faith were "brought near by his blood"; (2) Jesus "broke down the dividing wall of hostility"; (3) "in his flesh he has made both [previously alienated] groups into one"; and (4) he has overcome deadly rivalry by "putting to death [the] hostility" (Eph. 2:13–14, alt.). The closely paired ideas that it is *in Jesus' body* that hostility is put to death and opposing groups are forged into one new humanity recur in verse 16. Hostility is pictured not only as a wall that Jesus breaks down in his death, but also as an entity that Jesus, in his dying, kills. In his own body, Jesus absorbs the hostility that arises from the endless clash of rival claims; furthermore, his body (and by extension the body of the church as well) is the site where humanity is made one, living by grace, beyond all claims.

The metaphor of the toxin-absorbing, life-creating body of Jesus as the site of reconciliation is an arresting one. Theologian Paula Cooey seems to have something very much like this in mind when she writes of God's redemptive action in Jesus as

> ongoing divine creativity characterized as self-emptying imagination, continually making relations, things, and events up from the flesh, making these real in the flesh and repairing broken relations and things by making them differently—creativity from the inside out rather than the top down, so to speak.[9]

Embodied in Jesus is new creation in the making. Christ's own body becomes the seedbed and nourishment for a community that will likewise live a life that is whole in relation to God and all others.

Preaching Notes

The metaphor of the cross as God's act of reconciliation is developed by Presbyterian minister James Goodloe IV in a sermon on Ephesians 2:11–22 titled "Christ Has Broken Down the Wall!"[10] From the outset of this sermon, Goodloe makes clear that the gospel announces what already is—the new reality created in Christ; it is not merely a proposal. In light of the cross, the breaking down of dividing walls is an accomplished fact: the dividing walls of hostility *are already broken down*; this is the reality that the Gospel announces. The only question is whether we will honor this reality or attempt to erect again what Christ has decisively broken down. "It would be a crying and damnable shame," Goodloe tells his listeners, "for us to believe . . . the lie that Jesus Christ has not broken down the wall, . . . by continuing to honor the dividing wall of hostility."

Many of us are comfortable with a doctrine of reconciliation with God, but truth be told, far less comfortable with its corollary: reconciliation with whomever we take to be other, different, wrong-thinking, obstructive, not part of our crowd. But these two kinds of reconciliation, Goodloe insists, are inseparable: "Reconciliation to God comes in a package deal with reconciliation to each other. You cannot have one without the other!" The breaking down of walls "stands close to the heart of the gospel, not out at the edges. This . . . is what the work of Christ is all about." It certainly is a temptation, Goodloe observes, to imagine that the Ephesian situation was so removed from our own as to make Paul's announcement irrelevant. But "let it not be said of us . . . that we presumed our situation so unique as to be beyond the reach of the gospel!"[11]

In an especially illuminating part of the sermon, Goodloe briefly reviews the different understandings of the human predicament that have prevailed in past centuries. Death was the great threat and "overriding problem of human existence" in the first centuries of the church, but the medieval church focused on sin, while the twentieth century envisioned the fundamental crisis of human existence as meaninglessness. Today, however, says Goodloe, the core problem of human existence is fragmentation—fragmented lives, fragmented societies, a fragmented world.[12] To be sure, "the dividing wall of hostility is high, and wide, and long, and deep, and hard, and ancient, and impenetrable." Yet God's commitment to breaking it down is signified in no less than the cross. "Our choice is to honor the wall or to honor the gospel," says Goodloe. At this point in the sermon, Goodloe inserts an extensive quote from Martin Luther King Jr.'s "I Have a Dream" speech—stirring words that are clearly dear to Goodloe himself, which he is counting on to connect with the reality of those to whom he is preaching. "It is time to honor the dream, and to dishonor the wall," Goodloe announces.

Goodloe makes clear that it is not our job to overcome the walls of hostility; Christ has already done that. Instead, it is a question for us of structuring our common life in a manner that takes seriously the fact that the dividing walls are already down. "It is incumbent upon us, so far as it lies within our power," Goodloe concludes, "to structure our common life in ways that are in accord with the gospel of Jesus Christ and not in ways that are antithetical to it."[13]

Many a congregation needs to hear a sermon like Goodloe's. It is not hard for any congregation to call to mind the walls, visible or invisible, that divide their church fellowship, their town, or their city. Preachers need only name what the congregation knows already, all too well. However, the positive side of the metaphor of reconciliation needs to be developed in the sermon as vividly as the negative. We preachers often find it easier to analyze problems than celebrate possibilities in our preaching; but most congregations are far more inspired to action when we point to signs of the reign of God breaking out in their midst than they are by our dismal rehearsals of their failures and sins. A preacher can lift up specific examples inside the congregation and beyond, in the larger community, to show what it is like to live in the belief that dividing walls have already been broken down. Interestingly, young children know little of the dividing walls of race, gender, and class that structure the world of their parents. Also striking is the way that natural disaster or human tragedy can render previously significant community divisions null and void as all draw together for survival and support; only later do the old rivalries reassert themselves. Perhaps the most vivid images of the "one new humanity" forged in Christ's body are eucharistic: whether in urban storefront, country chapel, or city cathedral, every eucharistic feast is a foretaste of the community that lives without walls and beyond all claims.

A more visceral image of God's embodied commitment to "making relation, things, and events up from the flesh, making these real in the flesh" (to quote Cooey again) comes to expression in "Curse and Promise," a sermon by Marilyn McCord Adams. Using the Old Testament image of covenant ritual from Genesis 15, Adams envisions the way God bodily and redemptively engages the endemic hostility and abuse in human relationships. The sermon's central image is an aisle of split animal carcasses in the covenant ratification ceremony between God and Abraham. Through this aisle moves the smoking firepot, symbol of God's presence. Adams sketches the mysterious scene, with its aura of darkly primitive ritual, in a few strokes:

> Ritual reassurance, covenant-sealing ceremony, love affair gone legitimate, official business deal. Heifer, she-goat, ram, split down the middle; turtle dove and pigeon, necks wrung. Sundown, trance,

dread and darkness. Smoking fire pot, flaming torch and fiery pillar passing through the pieces. YHWH taking on himself the conditional curse of covenant vows. How sure are YHWH's promises? "Let it be to me as it is with these animals if I do not keep my word!"[14]

God ratifies God's promise to Abraham, but not for Abraham only, but for all who turn to God in faith.

Much of the time, Adams reminds us, our story is one of failure and wandering, breaking our promises, betraying and feeling betrayed ourselves. Yet astonishingly, what appears amid our dread and darkness is "Christ crucified, that flaming torch and fiery pillar, shining on with unquenchable light." Now "God in Christ crucified absorbs the curse— caricatured, distorted, ruined, hacked in two by others' rage."[15] This is the self-surrender of God to the curse of a broken covenant—regardless of which party may be the covenant breaker. For Adams, it is the Eucharist that makes palpable through bread and wine the promise of God, inscribed in body and blood, to absorb the curse of our hostility and make the covenant relationship whole:

> Here we offer ourselves, souls and bodies, our weary waiting, broken dreams, the hurt we suffered, the grief we've caused. Here with broken bread and poured out wine we show forth Christ crucified, that flaming torch and fiery pillar, passing through not over, becoming the sacrifice, turning it, us, into Christ's *glorified* body, into God's own self.[16]

Vividly, and with a striking economy of words, Adams sets forth in this sermon the death and resurrection of Jesus as that bodily event in which God absorbs violence and creates humanity anew.

The (Slain) Lamb Who Reigns

A less-familiar but striking metaphor that recalibrates our understanding of God's relation to violence is developed by Brian K. Blount in his African American cultural reading of the book of Revelation, *Can I Get a Witness? Reading Revelation through African American Culture.*[17] Here, the image of the slaughtered Lamb emerges as a metaphor for God's redemptive engagement with violent power. In Revelation 5 especially, but elsewhere in Revelation as well, Blount points out, "John provocatively pairs *Lamb* with the adjective *slaughtered*."[18] Slaughter, Blount tells us, literally means the exercise of power. It signifies the exercise, in fact, of the power of violence. The Lamb that has been slaughtered is a carcass, the ultimate symbol of victimhood and powerlessness. Yet, the writer of Revelation juxtaposes the image of the slaughtered Lamb with the divine throne in passage after passage (Blount cites no less than nineteen instances), setting up a new metaphor for divine power: the slaughtered Lamb that rules. This in itself is a metaphor—two unlike images drawn into a tensive, meaning-generating relation. The ruling/slaughtered Lamb metaphor is set into relation with Jesus' death, underscoring the paradox of divine power appearing as weakness, the weakness of death as the power that overcomes evil. Blount clarifies:

> The complete formulation, *slaughtered Lamb*, operates for John the way parables operated for Jesus, taking on qualities people expect, then overturning them. All of a sudden, Jesus' status as victim morphs into that of victor. It is as if the Lamb, acting exactly the way one expects a Lamb to act, or, in this case, to be acted upon, produces like a lion.[19]

Ultimately, for the writer of Revelation, the slaughtered Lamb becomes a figure of victory, reigning in a new heaven and earth. God's power of transformation, it seems, will not be obvious; in fact, God's power breaking out among us will look for all the world like a slaughtered Lamb—at least within this world that pursues its aims by violent domination. But, says Blount, "for John, weakness is the silver bullet that God fires out like a deadeye marksman against the scarcely exposed heart of cosmic and human evil. . . . Weakness is a weapon. Jesus deployed it on the cross," and, Blount continues, the weapon of weakness in a world that dominates through violence is not a onetime weapon, but the way of God's new world: "Jesus' followers must now trigger it with their lives."[20]

Blount underscores that a ruling-slaughtered-Lamb understanding of Jesus' suffering and death stands in stark contrast with the notion of Jesus' going to his death in voiceless, meek submission. In the black church, this latter idea of Jesus as submissive sufferer has too often encouraged believers to seek comfort in their faith, but to submit to violent systems *without* challenging them or pressing for them to be transformed. Embracing the slaughtered Lamb of Revelation commits us to struggle against violence and oppression, not to submit to it. True, the slaughtered-Lamb metaphor tells us that "a life committed to social transformation will entail struggle and perhaps even great suffering"; but John's Lamb is no icon of vulnerability. This is a "resistant Lamb."[21] Paradoxically, the slaughtered

Lamb "sLambs" ("slaughtered-lambs") its opposition.[22] The Lamb of Revelation undergoes violence—slaughter, in fact—but refuses to go down. This slaughtered Lamb lives and prevails, rendering powerless the powers that try to vanquish it by violence.

Blount is nothing if not a preacher; preachers can learn from Blount's cadences, which jump the gap from print to preaching in line after line. We can practically hear the "Amens!" rising from a congregation on its feet as Blount declares, "When you throw weakness around, worlds change. Empires fall. Justice rises."[23]

This is redemptive news to be preached; yet it is, above all, redemptive news to be lived, Blount insists. We would betray the intent of Blount's rereading of the slaughtered-Lamb metaphor if we were to reduce it to another interesting atonement "theory." Blount's dynamic language emerges out of a high-stakes rereading of Revelation grounded deep in the concrete reality of violence experienced by black Americans and their forebears. The slaughtered-Lamb metaphor, Blount contends, only fully discloses the dynamics of redemption when followers of Jesus face down powers that seem bent on their destruction and, like the slaughtered Lamb who prevails, refuse to go down.

Too often, the church has read John's apocalypse as a preview of the future, a decoder map for spectators who want to stay aloof from historical struggle and remain on the sidelines, waiting for God to draw the final curtain. Blount reminds us that Revelation was never meant to be read that way; it yields its meaning only when taken seriously as a call to political and social action. John's strange text is a rallying cry, summoning believers into the arena of ethical action amid forces of social and political violence, in the company of the slaughtered Lamb. Instead of watching the clouds for a literal slaughtered Lamb to materialize, Christians must focus on the present moment of struggle. They must follow in the slaughtered Lamb's way and take their place among the embattled ranks of the all-too-apparently weak, confident that God is already transforming the present precisely by "wreaking weakness."[24]

Preaching Notes

Ethicist Stanley Hauerwas, preaching on the fourth of the "seven last words" of Jesus from the cross ("My God, my God, why have you forsaken me?"), begins his sermon with a brief rehearsal of some of the names and dates that have become symbolic of horror: World War I;

Auschwitz; Hiroshima; Rwanda; September 11, 2001.[25] Humanly speaking, Hauerwas observes, it is little wonder that Jesus' cry of dereliction, of all the seven last words, strikes the deepest chord of recognition in many of us. Yet if we only understand the cry as comforting evidence that Jesus really *was* human after all, and therefore really understands our trouble, we understand too little about the cross—or about this cry.

If we take the cry of dereliction to be little more than an expression of Jesus' humanness and ability to sympathize with us, this may in fact be "an indication of our refusal, indeed our inability, to believe that this One who hangs on this obscure and humiliating cross is God."[26] Jesus is expressing far more than universal human anxiety in the face of death. If this is the cry of God's Messiah, argues Hauerwas, the cry testifies to God's being handed over in God's self to death for our sakes.

> This is not God becoming what God was not, but rather here we witness what God has always been. Here, as the Second Council of Constantinople put it, "one of the Trinity suffered in the flesh.". . . The cross . . . is not God becoming something other than God, is not an act of divine self-alienation; instead this is the very character of God's *kenōsis*—complete self-emptying made possible by perfect love.[27]

The cry of dereliction "and the cross itself, mean that the Father is to be found when all traces of power, at least as we understand power, are absent, that the Spirit's authoritative witness is most clearly revealed when all forms of human authority are lost; and that our God's power and authority is to be found exemplified in this captive under the sentence of death."[28]

The cry of dereliction troubles us, Hauerwas suggests, because we are anxious to "save and protect God from making a fool out of being God; but our attempts to protect God reveal how frightening we find a God who refuses to save us by violence. God is most revealed when he seems most hidden."[29] It is only by understanding that the Trinitarian God was fully present as the victim of violence on the cross that we come to terms with God as God is: the God who refuses to save by violence, a God slain and weak, who will achieve our deliverance not by perpetrating violence but only by undergoing it.

Jesus as Universal Scapegoat

In recent years some theologians have sought fresh understanding of the saving significance of Jesus' death by reconsidering it in light of what is known as "scapegoat" theory. The theory of scapegoat sacrifice, an observable social mechanism for controlling violence, was developed by anthropologist René Girard.[30] Theologian S. Mark Heim is among those who have explored the way that scapegoat theory can function, heuristically at least, to open up fresh understanding about the meaning of the cross.[31]

At the heart of human social relations, argued Girard, is a deep and endlessly repeated drama of violence in which a designated victim is chosen and then destroyed as a means for siphoning off dangerous levels of rivalrous violence in a society. Why should such murderous levels of violence exist? The source of the violence is basically envy, or what Girard calls "mimetic desire." The way it works is this: Agent A desires object X (which could be a possession, a sexual object, or anything else). Object X becomes desirable now to another agent, Agent B, simply because Agent A desires X. (Hence the "mimetic" nature of desire.) Violent competition for the object of desire escalates until a vendetta of vengeance murder is set in motion. Yet if this pattern of vengeance murder is allowed to continue, the clan (or larger social group) will be wiped out. This is when a scapegoat is selected—usually someone who is an outsider to the group, or someone in the group who seems "other" or "different"—and is assigned responsibility for the group's conflict. (By this time the whole business of competition between Agent A and Agent B over object X may have, in fact, been long since lost to memory.) Once the scapegoat has been destroyed, the rising pressure of violence and counterviolence is temporarily relieved, and social harmony is achieved—until the whole cycle of mimetic desire starts up again.

It is not difficult to bring to mind the ways this dynamic works, everywhere from the elementary school playground to clashes between rival ethnic groups in society. Kids on the playground teeter on the edge of a brawl over whose turn it is to play with the coolest ball in the bin; but just before that can happen, along comes the quiet kid who is somehow different—different in skin tone, or wearing different clothes, or not up to speed in math. Suddenly the former rivals are allies, ganged up against the selected victim, who is in for a pounding. Similar patterns at the level of religious, ethnic, and economic warfare are all too easy to detect. Brittle community or international relations can be resolved if the parties can identify a common enemy. As Mark Heim puts it:

> Scapegoating violence is the prototypical "good bad thing" in human culture, a calibrated dose of unjust violence that wards off wider,

unrestrained violence. Scapegoating is one of the deepest structures of human sin, built into our religion and our politics. It is demonic because it is endlessly flexible in its choice of prey and because it can truly deliver the good that it advertises.[32]

What happens, Heim proposes, if we reconsider the cross in light of Girard's thesis—or to put it another way, Girard's thesis in light of the cross? Heim examines a wide range of biblical texts, demonstrating that there is evidence in the Bible for a widespread human assumption that a designated sacrificial victim is necessary to achieve reconciliation between human beings and between human beings and the divine. The matter of God's stance toward the scapegoating process is presented ambiguously in the Old Testament, Heim observes. The choice of the designated victim— the "other," the outsider to the community—is sometimes displaced onto God. Biblical stories often follow a pattern, says Heim, that "begins with the escalation of mimetic conflict in human social life and ends with the reconciliation granted to the community when it enlists divine powers in unanimous violence against the outcast."[33] There is, however, another narrative that competes with this one. God also emerges as the one who gives the scapegoat a voice, who is the ally of scapegoated victims. Heim's readings of the Psalms and the book of Job, in particular, accent this dual portrait of God as a deity who on the one hand demands the sacrifice of victims, but who on the other hand sides with victims.

The cross, however, takes up the scapegoating drama and gives it a new and decisive twist: this time, God becomes the victim. In the death of Jesus, God participates in scapegoating violence in a manner that ends it. Part of the "magic" of the scapegoat mechanism, as Girard and his interpreters point out, is its secrecy. The participants do not "know," or at least pretend not to know, that what they are doing really *is* scapegoating. The great secret at the heart of the drama is that the violence unleashed on the scapegoat is not the scapegoat's fault; it is displaced violence. This is what participants in scapegoat violence do not see, because they cannot afford to see it; if they *did* see it, they would have to face their own violence—and their own guilt. So intolerable would that be that utterly devastating killing would be the result. And this is what the scapegoat mechanism is designed to prevent.

But at the cross, the innocence of the victim cannot quite be suppressed; the secret is out. Here, writes Heim, "the scapegoating process is stripped of its sacred mystery, and the collective persecution and abandonment are painfully illustrated for what they are, so that no one, including the disciples, . . . can honestly say afterward that they resisted the sacrificial tide."[34]

Heim shows that Jesus unmasks the scapegoat mechanism not only at the cross, but also in his teaching. The story that presents this unmasking most tellingly, for Heim, is the story of the woman caught in adultery (John 7:53–8:11). When Jesus bids the one without sin to cast the first stone, he breaks up the mob mentality that perpetrates scapegoat violence. This invitation by Jesus is "a differentiating one," says Heim. To take him up on it, individuals in the mob would have to step forward and bear individual responsibility for the violence. The power of scapegoating violence lies, however, in the safety of the crowd's anonymity. In scapegoating of the sort the women's accusers were practicing, "the logic of sacrifice pulls everyone together against the subject"; but Jesus forces the perpetrators of this would-be scapegoat sacrifice to identify themselves, and one by one they turn away. Guilt now attaches to each of those who could not declare themselves sinless and could not step forward. The scapegoat mechanism has been exposed.[35]

Jesus' death, the sacrifice to end sacrifice, exposes the scapegoat mechanism. Furthermore, says Heim, the fact of Jesus' resurrection siphons off, once for all, the guilty violence that has kept the gears of the machine turning. Raised by God, the scapegoat is acquitted of any charges against him. Oddly, those who murdered him are acquitted, too; they cannot be guilty of murder if the victim lives. Forgiven and free, those whom God has embraced no longer need the scapegoat machine. By entering into the scapegoating drama in the place of the victim, God unmasks and disarms it. Jesus is the "firstfruit" of the vindication of all victims.[36]

Heim acknowledges that a Girardian reading of the cross is vulnerable to two criticisms. First, unless anthropological data support the notion of the *universality* of the pattern of mimetic rivalry and scapegoating violence, the universal scope and significance of seeing Jesus as the ultimate and final scapegoat is diminished. Second, we can ask whether the simple fact that Jesus' death exposes to view the scapegoat mechanism can be said to fundamentally change the human condition. Is it not obvious that such scapegoating did not end with Jesus' resurrection? Can an event that is fundamentally epistemological produce salvation in an ontological sense?

Certainly, if it is a comprehensive, fully adequate *theory* of atonement we are after, then neither Girard nor Heim has given us such a theory. Yet the scapegoat paradigm tells us something profoundly revealing about human sin and its enslaving power. To recognize Jesus as the scapegoat who bears away the deadliness of endless, murderous human desire is compelling, because it connects the saving significance of Jesus' death to human sin and violence on multiple levels. Furthermore, the scapegoat paradigm accords with particular New Testament texts about Jesus' death. Romans 5:8–11 can be plausibly read in light of this metaphor ("if while we were enemies, we were reconciled to God through the death of his Son, much more surely, having been reconciled, will we be saved by his life"; v. 10). Ephesians 2:15–18, discussed earlier, also harmonizes with this metaphor.

Preaching Notes

Two sermons, one by Barbara Brown Taylor, the other by pastor Debbie Blue, a founding pastor of House of Mercy Church in St. Paul, Minnesota, demonstrate the disclosive power of the scapegoat metaphor in preaching.

In a sermon titled "The Myth of Redemptive Violence," Barbara Brown Taylor exposes and challenges redemptive violence along the lines traced by Girard and his interpreters.[37] Although she does not use René Girard's technical language, Taylor sketches his thesis of a myth of redemptive violence, showing how Jesus is a victim within an age-old story in which the problem of escalating violence is "resolved" by yet more violence. In a few deft strokes, Taylor exposes the irony in our widespread belief that "the only way the world can be saved is to get the weapons out of the hands of the hoodlums and into the hands of the righteous, who can be trusted to hurt bad guys only."[38] In everything from children's Saturday morning TV cartoons to international foreign policy, this notion is pervasive.

In his betrayal, trial, suffering, and death, as Taylor shows us, Jesus takes into himself all the violence flung at him and will not give back violence for violence.

> Jesus was killed for not buying into the myth of redemptive violence. He is testimony against our futile myth that counter-violence will put an end to violence. Day by day, he invites us to follow him . . . the one who fought back by refusing to fight back and who replaced the myth of redemptive violence with the truth of indestructible love. Here, then, is another way to redeem the world: not by killing off the troublemakers but by dying to violence once for all.[39]

Taylor interprets this image of the cross as primarily exemplary. Jesus, absorbing violence instead of falling prey to the myth that further violence (perpetrated, of course, by the "righteous") will make the world whole, gives us a path to follow. "Because he did, we can. He died to show us how. We live to show him we got the message."[40] The saving significance of the cross for a violent world is as a strategy for changed behavior.

Pastor Debbie Blue's sermon develops the scapegoat metaphor in even greater detail than does Taylor's and then allows it to function as a lens into human experience that discloses how God is redemptively engaged to detoxify human conflict. Blue begins by alerting her listeners that she is about to tell them three versions of a story that is familiar and is, in a sense, the same story, happening over and over—"sometimes it seems like it's the *only* story. You hear it over and over and see it over and over and tell it and make it and do it over and over."[41] In each story, two parties at odds with one another achieve reconciliation by focusing their hostility on a third party, an "other" or outsider. Finding and blaming a victim is a way human beings have of dealing with the dangerously volatile rivalries between them, from the second-grade classroom to the negotiation of social and economic conflicts at the community-wide level.

In contrast to these three scapegoat stories, Blue tells us, Mark's Passion story is a "different" story—a story in which Jesus does not resort to the age-old ploy of dealing with the conflict in which he is enmeshed by turning everyone against someone else, a common victim. On trial for his life, Jesus could have triggered that story, says Blue:

> Jesus could have unified the crowd so easily against the religious leaders or the Romans, . . . or the Jews against the Romans. . . . But this really isn't that story. It's not the story of God unifying God's people against an *other*. It's the story of all the people, the strong and the weak and the good and the bad, the religious and the pagans, all the people, everyone unifying against Jesus Christ, the incarnation of God's love in the world.[42]

On one level, of course, it looks as if we are watching just another repetition of the same old story—with Jesus as the scapegoat of the moment. "From this end," says Blue, "it looks as though the scapegoating machine is running full on, smooth and strong." But in fact,

> Jesus in his death and resurrection does the farthest thing from oiling the wheels of that machine. He breaks it to pieces. He becomes

the scapegoat for everyone to define themselves over against; he becomes utterly vulnerable to all of them, all of us.[43]

Blue is alert as well to the fact that the scapegoat metaphor potentially leaves us with a purely exemplarist, "subjective" notion of the significance of the cross, so that Jesus' exposure of our scapegoating only "counts" if we "get it" and take it to heart. She presses on to interpret this act of God's absorption of scapegoating violence as an *objective* redemptive divine action: "Could it be that Jesus, the incarnation of God's love in the world, . . . comes for us all? To scoop us up out of the death-dealing, death-making monotony of the machine and into the love of God?"[44]

Summarizing in a vocabulary that hovers close to Girard's own, Blue concludes: "Jesus dies, not to convict us of our crime, but to scoop us up for life lived and fed by a whole different fuel, something completely other than rivalry, scapegoating, vengeance, and violence."[45]

Blue's sermon shows that the scapegoat metaphor, while not explicitly present in Scripture, is exhibited narratively in the Gospels, particularly in Mark's passion story. Both Taylor and Blue demonstrate the power of the scapegoat metaphor when it is drawn alongside human social dynamics that a congregation will readily recognize. There is something about the scapegoating pattern that makes deep sense of the human condition, whether the violence that cries out for redemptive address is taking place at the domestic level, at the community level of social and political rivalries and conflicts, or at the level of global, international relations.

If Heim is right, the only reason we continue the scapegoat drama at all is because we do not see that, this side of the cross, it is no longer needed: we already have all we need. We are already whole, already forgiven.

In a world where the assault of violence on human bodies and minds continues ceaselessly around the clock, preachers owe it to themselves and their congregations to relate the violent death of Jesus in constructive ways to this endemic feature of twenty-first-century existence. Our congregations do not need or expect from us a sophisticated theological theory that explains fully how the God we have come to know in the crucified One is related to violence. Excellent work on the subject continues to be done by able theologians.[46] As preachers, we can simply begin by rereading the tradition of the cross from the place where our congregations live and struggle—specifically amid the world's relentless

violence—calling a variety of metaphors of the cross into play in our sermons. Acknowledging the modesty of metaphor and its exploratory
rather than explanatory function, preacher and congregation together
can press toward new insight and imaginatively discover how it is that
the God made known to us in One who suffered violence has entered
redemptively into our violent world. God has come among us in Jesus,
the violently crucified One, in order to absorb, unmask, and disarm this
world's deep patterns of hostility and violence and to renew it in peace.

6

Jesus' Death as Sacrifice

Can This Metaphor Be Saved?

Sacrifice, one of the most commonly used metaphors for interpreting Jesus' death since New Testament times, has become one of the most controversial today. Lutheran theologian Paul Fiddes observes that "'sacrifice' was probably the first image by which the Christian community interpreted its experience of salvation."[1] Sacrifice, a familiar practice in ancient cultures, proved to be both a powerful and portable metaphor for the dispersed and culturally diverse communities that grew up as a result of the early Christian mission. Anglican priest and theologian John Moses goes so far as to say that "the notion of the death of Jesus as a sacrifice is so significant within the New Testament that no theory of atonement can stand within the Christian tradition if it does not incorporate the elements of sacrifice."[2] For centuries, sacrifice language has been associated with Jesus' death in hymns and liturgies as well. Every week thousands of worshipers pray such words as these from *The Book of Common Prayer* of the Episcopal Church: "He [Jesus] stretched out his arms upon the cross, and offered himself, in obedience to your will, a perfect sacrifice for the whole world."[3]

However, as we have already seen, feminist and womanist theologians express concern that associating sacrifice with Jesus' death has had an adverse impact on some believers, particularly women, and especially minority women. In the days of North American slavocracy, womanist Delores Williams reminds us, slaves were encouraged to embrace a piety centered on Jesus' sacrificial, substitutionary death. This lent an aura of the sacred to black slave women's service as surrogate caretakers, or even sexual partners, in white households. When preachers and theologians continue to speak of Jesus' death as sacrifice, Williams contends, they unwittingly encourage contemporary women, too, to accept self-diminishing patterns in home and workplace.[4]

Not all womanists agree with Williams's assessment. JoAnne Marie Terrell argues that a more positive interpretation of Jesus' death as sacrifice is possible for African Americans than Williams envisions. Black women who have lived and labored sacrificially so their children can thrive, acquire education, and better their lives have often testified that they have found meaning and inspiration by identifying with Jesus' sacrificial self-giving. Their testimony indicates that suffering and sacrifice need not be regarded as ends in themselves; instead, suggests Terrell, these are redeemable experiences, manifesting on one hand the brokenness of the human condition, and on the other the determination of God to overcome such enslaving, spirit-denigrating brokenness.[5]

But preachers face challenges in addition to overcoming the problems Williams and others have identified. Fiddes warns that theologians and preachers who interpret Jesus' death in terms of sacrifice must take into account the fact that sacrifice language has suffered "semantic slippage" since the early centuries of Christianity; sacrifice motifs have taken on a secular life of their own in Western culture. "We may fail to perceive that the word *sacrifice* has not 'stayed still,'" remarks Fiddes, "or we may mistake the way in which it has moved, from the time when the early Christians used it as a way of understanding the effect of the death of Christ in their lives."[6]

Contemporary associations with sacrifice range from the heroic to the commercial. Soldiers who die in battle as well as firefighters and police who die in the line of duty are said to have "made the ultimate sacrifice." On the other hand, retailers trumpet year-end "sacrifice" sales to make room for new stock, and dieters are encouraged to "sacrifice" the occasional dessert in order to achieve the perfect shape. When popular notions of sacrifice, particularly sentimental or trivial ones, have made their way into a congregation's thinking, just what the preacher means when she calls Jesus' death a "sacrifice" can be murky indeed.

Yet sacrifice motifs are quite prominent in biblical literature and in a long tradition of atonement language in both East and West. Preachers and their congregations need to make sense of this faith-shaping and faith-informing tradition. There is good reason, then, to ask whether this family of metaphors can function more positively, without either glorifying self-diminishment and suffering or reducing Jesus' death to an act of heroism.

IDEAS OF SACRIFICE IN THE BIBLE AND ANCIENT CULTURES

In the religions of the ancient world, including Judaism, sacrifice was so widely practiced and intuitively understood that sacrifice rituals are described in ancient texts like the Bible with minimal explanation about their intent or what participants believed about their efficacy. In many Old Testament texts, therefore, the meaning of prescribed sacrifices is not spelled out in any detail. Many types of sacrifice are mentioned in connection with different acts of worship, communal and individual. What we actually find in these texts is not a single, univocal sacrifice metaphor, but something that resembles a web of related practices and associated meanings. Along with differences of procedure, interpreters detect subtle shades of difference concerning the likely intention and effects of an array of sacrificial actions.

By contrast, the ideas about sacrifice that shape many twenty-first-century congregations' imagination are relatively narrow. Two in particular are generously represented in popular revival-tradition hymns from the late nineteenth and early twentieth centuries: (1) the idea that Jesus' blood is a cleansing agent that washes away the "stain" of sin, and (2) the belief that Jesus is a sacrificial victim who accepts the punishment of death so we will not have to. Interestingly, these particular ideas about the efficacy of sacrifice are difficult to establish on the basis of the Old Testament sacrifice texts that inform Christian understanding. It is crucial, then, for us to reexamine what biblical texts say—and do not say—about sacrifice before we can take up this metaphor of redemption in helpful ways.

In Old Testament texts, rituals using the blood of sacrificial animals are said to "make atonement" for sin, but it is participation in the sacrificial ritual *as a whole* that "makes atonement," not the blood, specifically. (See, among many other texts, Lev. 9:7.) Other texts speak of sprinkling oil and blood as symbols of consecration, as in Leviticus 8:30, where Moses consecrates Aaron, his sons, and their priestly vestments. While washings were indeed associated with sacrifice, one was washed with water, certainly not blood. Although we read in 1 John 1:7 that "the blood of Jesus Christ . . . cleanses us from all sin," we are probably pushing the metaphor too far if we hasten to imagine "a fountain filled with blood," as a popular nineteenth-century gospel hymn puts it.[7] This is likely a case of a metaphor's having been overextended and overliteralized.

The Old Testament provides even less support for the idea that the point of a sacrifice was for the sacrificial victim to die so that the worshiper would not have to. In fact, in the Old Testament text where the association between sin-bearing and sacrifice is most explicitly drawn, Leviticus 16, the sin-bearing scapegoat *does not die*; the *living* goat is driven out into the wilderness, bearing the community's sins (Lev. 16:10, 21–22). As theologian Peter Schmiechen points out, "The victim does not die vicariously for sinners; the death of the victim is not a substitute for a death penalty pronounced against a sinner."[8]

In ancient sacrificial rituals, the role of the animal was not so much substitutionary as representative. Ancient cultures that practiced animal sacrifice believed that a bond of identification existed between offerer and offering, an identification often symbolized by the offerer laying hands on the head of the animal being sacrificed.[9] Cultures across the ancient world understood the act of sacrifice to represent the gifting of the essence of the self to the deity, resulting in communion with the divine being. Within this framework of meaning, the accent in sacrifice falls on offering the *gifting* of life, not the violent *taking* of life.[10] Similarly, in many Old Testament contexts, the sacrificial animal represents the gift to God of the worshiper's or community's life; it does not represent substitute death.

Moreover, in ancient religious thought, the essence of life was in the blood of a living being; thus the outpouring of the animal's blood in sacrifice rituals underscored the offering of life to God. The point was not the "violence" of bloodshed; in fact, the blood was let as humanely as possible. There is no reason to suppose that blood was a death symbol; rather, Leviticus 17:11 seems to state quite the opposite: "For the life of the flesh is in the blood, . . . as life, it is the blood that makes atonement." This understanding that blood symbolizes life and is life-giving has been largely lost in the imagination of most Christians today.

In Jewish worship, what was at stake was to make whole the relationship with God by symbolizing through the gift of a perfect animal the gifting of one's life, complete and unblemished, in covenant fidelity to God. Only gradually in the Jewish sacrificial context did emphasis shift toward the expiation of sin, although pagan cultic religions tended to stress propitiating an angry deity through sacrifice, or using sacrifice as a means of persuading the deity to avert natural disaster, defeat at the hands of enemies, illness, or spiritual evil.

By the time of Jesus, sacrifice had taken on additional meanings, thanks to the influence of Hellenistic culture. The conceptual paradigm of a representative death "for the people" by a heroic personage was not unknown in the ancient world by that time.[11] Thus by the first century, notes historian Edward Hulmes, "the meaning shifts in general usage to denote heroic attitudes and costly acts which have no transcendent reference of a specifically religious nature."[12] Early Christian writings reveal that this concept of heroic and representative self-sacrifice was incorporated into Christian interpretation of Jesus' death.

New Testament scholars debate whether or not sacrifice metaphors are central in Paul's interpretation of the death of Jesus. J. D. G. Dunn argues that, while sacrifice was by no means Paul's only frame of reference, the idea figured prominently in his thought, citing such passages as Romans 3:25 ("God put [Christ Jesus] forward as a sacrifice of atonement") and 1 Corinthians 5:7 ("Our paschal lamb, Christ, has been sacrificed"). Colin Gunton warns, however, that wherever the sacrifice metaphor is invoked in the New Testament, whether in Pauline texts or elsewhere, we do well to remember that we are dealing with the openness and tensiveness of metaphorical meaning, not a relationship of literal, one-for-one equivalence between the event of Jesus' death and practices of sacrifice. Thus Gunton reminds us, "We should not expect all of the biblical expressions to say precisely the same thing, but to contribute at different levels and in different places to our understanding of the many-sided event."[13]

SAVING SACRIFICE METAPHORS

For preachers, the issue may not be so much *whether* to speak of Jesus' death in relation to sacrifice, but *how*. Sacrifice language occupies such a prominent place in the biblical tradition and in centuries of Christian interpretation of Jesus' death that it is difficult to imagine how preachers can completely ignore this web of metaphors. Homiletician L. Susan Bond makes the important observation that "christologies must be plausibly related to the language and the symbols that congregations recognize." Theologian Sallie McFague also suggests that our theological language needs to have "demonstrable continuity" with Christian tradition.[14]

Preachers can take specific steps to dispel myths and misimpressions about sacrifice and reclaim more positive meanings. First, we can simply introduce the congregation to biblical texts that speak of sacrifice.

As our brief survey of some of these texts indicates, sacrifice was undertaken on many occasions, for many purposes, and with many different meanings. This insight alone can help to dislodge mistaken or narrow understandings of sacrifice that lead, in turn, to distorted interpretations of Jesus' death.

Second, preachers can challenge and correct less-helpful notions of sacrifice inherited from hymns or other popular Christian sources.[15] One could juxtapose an Old Testament text about sacrifice with the text of a gospel hymn, raising questions about what each of these says, and bringing into the sermon the idea of sacrifice as superabundant gift, rather than substitute death. Third, we need to recognize that the term "sacrifice" has taken on a set of meanings in popular culture as a whole that may or may not be helpful for Christian reflection. Preachers need to make clear, for example, that Jesus' death is more than an act of heroism. Moving as it is to read stories of those who have risked or given their lives in order to save others from fire or disaster, we are dealing with something more than this when we make Christian sense of Jesus' death.

When preachers reenvision Jesus' death as a creative act of life and an expression of compassion, rather than self-diminishment or passive acquiescence to abuse, its meaning as an act of sacrifice can become the basis for creative and life-giving patterns of Christian belief and practice. In this way, the language congregations hear from the pulpit will have continuity with the biblical tradition and with liturgy, but at the same time, unhelpful ideas can be dispelled and new, more life-giving ones put in their place.

At the level of theological interpretation, three decisive changes in the way preachers speak of sacrifice will do much, over time, to "save" the sacrifice metaphor from misconstrual or neglect.

1. First, preachers can challenge understandings of sacrifice as a matter of appeasement or payment of a death penalty, emphasizing instead sacrifice as creative self-"gifting." The point here is to undo some unhelpful historical developments in our understanding of sacrifice and to relocate the foundation of our understanding in concepts of the gifting of life, not the destruction of life.

Over time, notes New Testament scholar Frances Young, Christian interpretations of Jesus' death within the horizon of sacrifice became increasingly narrow, losing sight of the life-symbolizing, gift-giving, communion-creating aspects of sacrifice and stressing the expiatory value of blood or the notion of appeasing divine wrath.[16] The dominance of propitiatory ideas in popular theology, says Young, "led to inconsistent statements: God is love, God is angry; God sent Christ, Christ placated God. The idea produced an unhappy picture of the divine Father and Son acting in opposition to one another."[17] Connecting sacrifice narrowly with propitiatory notions of sacrifice, argues theologian Ian Bradley, "is hugely to confine and diminish its power and scope; it also gives a largely negative and reactive character to the purpose and character of God. . . . The principle of sacrifice in the divine as well as in human life . . . points to a much more fundamental and positive impulse at the heart of the being of God—a self-giving which is incarnational as much as atoning."[18] Colin Gunton notes that even John Calvin, whose name is so often associated with penal, expiatory, and propitiatory interpretations of the cross, underscored that it is the whole of Jesus' embodied *life* that is sacrificial. It is in Jesus' willingness to be clothed in flesh to live his life as a consistent, sacrificial offering of his whole being to God, by which Jesus makes whole the communion of human beings with God.[19]

Many theologians and historians agree that it is time to restore emphasis in Christian imagination to the creative, self-gifting trajectory of sacrifice, rather than the bloody destruction of life that has more to do with appeasement of an angry deity. While these latter meanings are evident in some later Jewish interpretation of the efficacy of sacrifice, they have dominated discussion of New Testament references to Jesus' death as a sacrifice, obscuring the idea that in sacrifice, one's very self is given or "handed over." It is crucial for preachers and teachers to emphasize, especially when dealing with Old Testament texts about sacrifice, that the shed blood of the gifted animal symbolized not destruction, but the treasured gift of life. Sacrifice signified the communion-creating, life-giving offering of the core self of the worshiper to God.

Jesus gives his whole life sacrificially in the sense of the donation of his very self, in his ministry and in his death, toward both humanity and God. The Gospel of Luke preserves the tradition of Jesus, characterizing his manner of life and death as an act of self-donation ("This is my body, which is given for you," Luke 22:19). Theologian Kathryn Tanner suggests that we reinterpret the incarnation as a whole, including Jesus' saving death, as expressive of "God's super-abundant self-giving."[20] By "assuming" our human life into God's self through the Word, Jesus Christ, God overcomes our failures and our lack within a mission of inexhaustible self-giving. This sacrificial self-donation characterizes Jesus' whole life, not exclusively his death.[21] Rethinking sacrifice this way not only accords better with many biblical texts about sacrifice, but also overcomes the problem of some atonement language appearing to disconnect Jesus' death from his life. The sacrificial nature of Jesus' death was the fulfillment of the superabundant, life-restorative nature of Jesus' entire life.

2. A second adjustment preachers can make as they draw connections between the cross and sacrifice is to *reverse the direction of the sacrificial self-gift* **made at the cross, so that we see clearly that** *God gives God's own life,* **to us and for us.** Anglican theologian John Moses emphasizes that in the death of Jesus, the trajectory of sacrificial gift-giving is radically reversed. At the cross, God is handed over to humanity. "God gives himself—hands himself over—to the pattern of life and death and life," writes Moses. The customary sacrificial terms are reversed to establish human-divine communion. Jesus as God's representative to humanity is given over to humanity, thus transgressing and overturning the assumed vector of sacrifice and proper sacrificial procedure. Jesus' self-givenness introduces an entirely new dynamic into human-divine relations.[22] Paul Fiddes likewise underscores the *violation* of sacrificial cultic norms in Jesus' death:

> Indeed the application of sacrificial terms to a person who is despised and rejected bursts open the categories of sacrifice altogether. . . . While the expiatory victim was meant to be a sacred object set apart from ordinary use, pure and unblemished in appearance, this victim is disfigured by suffering and "makes his grave with the wicked." . . . The very circumstances of the death question the common understanding of sacrifice.[23]

S. W. Sykes argues similarly, observing that since "God is present and involved in what had been deemed impure," Jesus embodies a new vision of divine-human relationship in which God is self-given to humanity as the basis of human-divine communion, not the reverse.[24]

In other words, Jesus' death, to the extent that it is a sacrifice, *radically reorders* sacrifice. New Testament scholar A. N. Chester presses toward an even more radical conclusion as he rereads sacrifice language in the book of Hebrews. He suggests that we read this epistle as a treatise arguing for the abandonment of not only temple sacrifice on the part of Jewish Christians, but also of the sacrificial system as a paradigm for interpreting human-divine relations. Jesus' death "fulfills" sacrifice, suggests Chester; Jesus' death is the *end* of sacrifice as we have known it. God's glad and complete self-giving is the basis of human-divine relations.[25] Within such a framework, sacrifice becomes transformative, creative self-donation. To live (or die) sacrificially is to render oneself vulnerable for the sake of the other. In Jesus, even God does not act from afar, aloof, with God's being held intact; God becomes vulnerably engaged with us, extending and offering God's own being and life to restore our life.

3. Third, preachers can bring into their sermons *new images of sacrifice that resonate with both the biblical witness and contemporary culture.* Feminist theologian Mary J. Streufert, seeking a "soteriology of restoration," rereads sacrifice imagery from her own social location as a woman and, specifically, one who has given birth to and raised children. Drawing on her experiences of pregnancy and motherhood as the point of departure for fresh thinking about sacrifice, Streufert develops the image of maternal sacrifice as a redemptive motif that can illuminate the sense in which Jesus gives himself, sacrificially, to give humanity life.

Contrasting violent, death-for-life motifs of sacrifice with the life-for-life motif of motherhood, Streufert suggests that the sacrifices involved in pregnancy and motherhood are *generative* sacrifices: they are life poured out to another to generate life. Streufert writes, "Physical and existential sacrifice does not always involve physical death. I am interested in the life-sacrifice of motherhood and how the life-for-life model inherent to the mother-child relationship might offer us an alternative model of sacrifice useful for christological interpretation."[26] Likewise, Streufert suggests, Jesus contributes to humanity abundant life-giving, creative energy. This makes the outpouring of our energies, physical and emotional, to nurture and sustain life the central meaning of sacrifice rather than violence and heroic death. Death is only sacrificial and meaningful if it comes about as one engages in a generative, sacrificial manner of life.[27] Generativity, not heroic death, is the true imitation of Christ.

The maternal image for sacrifice emphasizes its life-giving efficacy and also resonates with such New Testament texts as Luke 13:34, where Jesus laments over Jerusalem and characterizes God in maternal language. Paul, too, draws on maternal imagery when he speaks of feeding his congregations (1 Cor. 3:2; 1 Thess. 2:7). Over the centuries, Christians have turned to the image of maternal self-giving as a metaphor of sacrifice that helps us understand the self-outpouring of Jesus. Early Christians treasured the eucharistic image of the mythic pelican plucking the flesh of its own breast to feed its young. Centuries later, Julian of Norwich utilized an image daring as much in our time as in hers, that of Jesus as a nursing mother.

SIN, SACRIFICE, AND SUBSTITUTION

An enlarged view of sacrifice can help us avoid the pitfalls of strictly penal interpretations of Jesus' death and yet allow us to recognize the sense in which Jesus bears, with us and for us, divine judgment against sin.

Jesus assumes our human condition—and that includes our sin; but Jesus is no more the substitute "target" for punishment than sacrificed animals in Old Testament sacrifices were. Rather, fulfilling and yet transcending the patterns of Old Testament sacrifice, Jesus representatively bears sin with and for us. Jesus is humanity's representative; assuming the full burden of our humanity, he bears sin's consequences on our behalf and for our deliverance. Sin's consequences include the fact that God's nature—God's righteousness and justice—are by definition set against sin and evil. This "set-against-ness" toward sin is what we experience as God's judgment against sin and evil; and this is the sense in which at the cross Jesus bore God's judgment against sin.

Jesus, fully human with us, hands himself over to God without reserve, giving himself over to the set-against-ness of God's nature toward sin. But, as theologian Kathryn Tanner memorably puts it, God's superabundant nature is such that, as God takes to God's self the human condition in the Word made flesh, an economy of debt is overcome by the divine economy of overflowing grace.[28]

Working with a revised understanding of sacrifice, preachers can guide their congregations toward more helpful ways of understanding the relationship of Jesus' death to human sinfulness. Many Christians, especially North American Christians from evangelical faith communities, tend to speak of the difference that Jesus makes for sinners in terms such as being delivered from eternal spiritual death, being forgiven, or having sin's stain washed away by Jesus' blood. These models and metaphors are strongly associated with the penal substitutionary model of atonement discussed in chapter 2, although elements of sacrificial language are frequently overlaid on this basic paradigm.

Thinking about sacrifice in a manner that accents Jesus' superabundant giving rather than notions of substitute dying helps us to rethink not only the nature of sacrifice, but also the nature of sin itself. Metaphors of sin as "debt" (paid off at the cross by a divinely engineered legal settlement) or as "stain" (expunged by the application of blood) have their place if care is taken to emphasize the limitations of these metaphorical expressions. Neither of these alone is large enough or complex enough to help us gain a sufficiently complex and nuanced understanding of the nature of sin, or to point, in turn, to a correspondingly large vision of salvation.

We can neither speak adequately of sin nor speak adequately of the saving significance of the cross if we imagine that sin is merely an individual matter of succumbing to moral temptation and do not recognize its complex, systemic nature and the way that political and cultural patterns both fuel and mask it. Sin certainly includes individual selfishness, deceit, envy, covetousness, and the rest. But there is little hope that we will understand the roots of our moral failures unless we also recognize that Jesus' death exposes sin that is social and systematic, so deeply rooted in our shared ways of life that we are blind to it. Racism and sexism, prejudice toward the aging or those with disability of differing kinds, measuring others' worth by wealth and social influence rather than character—these are all patterns that distort and dismember human community. Playing on the insecurities of others to sell people things they do not need, abusing our power at home or in the workplace, hardening our hearts against suffering, and colluding in global marketing patterns that siphon money and resources away from vulnerable countries to benefit the richest—these are sins that diminish our lives as well as those of others. Salvation thought of as simple debt-cancellation is too small a model of redemption to get to the roots of such sin. Sacrifice reenvisioned as self-donation for the well-being of all exposes sin not only at the individual level, but also at the communal and global level as well.

What is sacrificial about Jesus' life and death is that Jesus pours out the superabundance of his life into our life, overcoming our death with life, lack with abundance, debt with grace. Once we understand this, we are better able to identify something essential about sin, too: sin is a withholding of ourselves, our abundance, our life. Sinfulness is what comes from the stingy, fearful, consumptive self that will stop at nothing in its self-absorption. Jesus, as the representative human one of God's restored creation, reverses—both in his representative, substitutionary living and in his representative, substitutionary dying—the centripetal, self-absorbed direction of our lives. His unstinting self-donation overcomes human sinfulness and its effects, delivering us from the deathliness of life lived for the sake of that small, stingy, embattled, self-aggrandizing self that can never get enough—enough power, enough possessions, enough sense of safety, enough satisfaction or adulation or belovedness.

Baptized into Jesus Christ, we live forgiven—"fore"-given, Christ-given—lives. We are handed over to God and each other as Jesus was handed over to God and to us. To be "in Christ" is to be actively given over, in our worship and in our witness, to life-giving life, living out of an economy of abundance as Jesus did, no longer acting out of our fear of scarcity, but living creative, imaginative lives that overflow in generous, enduring love for God and neighbor.

Opportunities abound for preachers to reinterpret sacrifice in their sermons. The hymns and liturgies of many churches include frequent references to sacrifice, and reflection on these liturgical elements can be very helpful to congregations. Celebrating the Lord's Supper provides an ever-present opportunity to augment, challenge, or overturn limited understandings of sacrifice. Holy Week preaching also lends itself to sermons that engage sacrifice metaphors. The preacher with the congregation can reflect critically on the language of hymns and liturgies, drawing both of these into dialogue with fresh interpretations of sacrifice that stress life-giving self-donation rather than ideas of penal destruction of life and erasure of the self.

Jesus' living and dying have set new terms for sacrifice that transcend both the semantics of ancient sacrifice rituals and contemporary political and cultural rhetoric. The outcry of sinful humanity for cleansing, forgiveness, and new life is met by the world-altering, radical generosity of the self-giving of God.

PREACHING NOTES: CREATIVE USES OF SACRIFICE METAPHORS IN PREACHING

A collection of sermons by Christian ethicist and labor activist Toyohiko Kagawa, published in 1935, exhibits a remarkable awareness of the semantic range of the term "sacrifice." Some of Kagawa's sermons draw on quite traditional ideas about sacrifice.[29] Yet in others, Kagawa brings the motif of sacrifice together with human experience in ways that reveal the life-for-the-sake-of-more-life motif emphasized by Mary J. Streufert.

In a sermon titled "The Cross as Truth," Kagawa alerts his listeners to the diversity of metaphors that Paul uses to express the meaning of the cross:

> Paul, in explaining the Cross, used a figure of speech which would attract the attention of merchants. He likened the transformation of Christian conversation to the process of barter and explained that redemption was one of the underlying principles of barter or exchange. He talks of buying back something which you have sold.

At another time he uses the figure of a peace being declared between armies which have been fighting each other on the field of battle. Again he uses the figure of a person acting as a mediator for those who have been dragged into court. Again he uses the illustration of the priest offering sacrifices in the temple, and likens the suffering of Christ on the cross to this rite. Thus Paul uses figures of speech drawn from all walks of life.[30]

In his sermons, Kagawa frequently explores the pertinence of the sacrifice image, especially the symbolism of the shedding of blood. At some points, Kagawa follows a fairly traditional path in envisioning sacrifice as a mode of Christian behavior. As we have noted, to preach, as Kagawa does at one point, that "when self has been extinguished, for the first time I return to real living," is decidedly unhelpful for women and others who struggle for any sense of selfhood or self-esteem.[31]

Yet at other points, Kagawa finds startlingly fresh meaning in the symbolism of sacrifice and in blood as a source of life. In a sermon titled "The Cross and Social Movements," Kagawa's contemporized rethinking of the significance of blood in relationship to sacrifice is remarkable and creative. He downplays notions that the literal shedding of blood is in some sense mysteriously "required" to expiate human guilt. Rather, Kagawa emphasizes a contemporary understanding of blood as the gift of life, emphasizing its properties to heal and restore the body:

> The blood is constantly circulating in the human body; if there is any injury anywhere, blood repairs the damage. We call this regenerative process anagenesis, but that means merely that we possess powers of repair and renewal as well as powers of growth. This is the duty of the blood.[32]

Kagawa likens Christian disciples' self-giving for the restoration of society to the power of the blood in the body to restore and heal: "Those who have thought deeply on [Christ's] love are the most useful to society and serve society as blood serves the body."[33] Kagawa continues, "Love has this restorative power; it does the work of the blood. This work of the blood is called in Christian teaching, the Cross."[34]

Kagawa compares Christian discipleship to the "work of the blood" as a symbol of social transformation:

> Well, then, if the blood has this function in the body, what is the work of those who represent the blood in society? It is their function to offer their lives as a sacrifice in order to serve others. . . . Take for

instance a labor union which makes an unsuccessful attempt to win some advantage from capitalism. . . . If the members of the union would hold together, no matter if they were defeated, and regardless of what sort of ill-treatment they received, or how cruelly they were punished, they would be fulfilling the work of the blood. Unless there is conscious acceptance of the work of the blood, unless there is a conscious willingness to atone for the faults of others, there is no true union.[35]

Like Christ, Christians are called to contribute healing energy to situations that require it:

The reality of love is the blood. Love must live again. It must wait till it lives again. . . . Those who have been saved through the blood of the Cross must from now on live the life of the blood; they must live the life of the Cross.[36]

Elsewhere, Kagawa elaborates on the life-giving qualities of blood:

The action of blood is universal; it functions throughout the body, feeding the nerve tissues, the digestive organs, the bones, the muscles and circulating throughout the whole system, having the power to restore any part of it. It is the same with love. Love is endowed with the power to redeem and heal throughout the past, present, and future, every part of the whole. The supreme manifestation of that love is the blood which Christ shed on the Cross. We believe it to be the manifestation of his love and are enabled to believe in the forgiveness of past sins and the healing of past offences.[37]

Throughout, Kagawa has avoided treating Christ's shed blood as a literal cleansing agent, as if bloodletting itself were the point. The blood represents the self-giving love of God in Christ—and *it is this self-gift that is the healing agent*, not the blood itself. Christ's shedding of blood represents his free gift of his life to the end that human beings would be set free from social oppression. Kagawa characterizes Christ's self-gift as that act in which Jesus "met the responsibility of the human face towards God—the gift of ourselves to God."[38] He celebrates sacrificial offering of one's energies to God for the sake of the world's renewal not on the basis of some misguided principle of self-erasure, but specifically because he sees such sacrificial self-gift as necessary if Christians are to become agents of real social transformation.

———

Preaching a few weeks after the terrorist attacks of September 11, 2001, Episcopal preacher Fleming Rutledge spoke of the cross-shaped beams found amid the wreckage at Ground Zero, the site where the World Trade Center towers collapsed. Setting the cross before her listeners from the beginning of the sermon, Rutledge declares, "The Cross of Christ is the only symbol that matches the devastation of Ground Zero."[39] She reminds her listeners of the much-repeated story about how, as workers were escaping the towers, the firefighters were determined to go up, one after another—up into the hell of smoke, flame, and horror above. Rutledge continues, "This has been the single most powerful piece of testimony to come from the center of the cataclysm. Why is that? Because sacrifice for the sake of others is the most powerful thing there is."[40] Rutledge then speaks of individuals last seen alive helping the injured or helping others to escape, as well as the brave souls on Flight 93 who attacked their hijackers, preferring to risk death than to see even more lives taken. And yet, Rutledge reminds her listeners, these larger-than-life stories are not the only stories to be told and remembered; she gathers up, as well, the hundreds of thousands of small acts of kindness and courage—such as Christians escorting Muslims to the supermarket, lest they be harrassed—that are also worthy of celebration.[41]

Rutledge concludes, "Each of these works of mercy is a sign of the Cross raised over the ruins." Because "'Christ has died, Christ is risen, Christ will come again,' . . . cross-shaped acts of Christian courage, no matter how small, testify to the coming Day of the Lord's ultimate triumph over evil."[42] The certainty for which many hungered in the days following September 11, Rutledge declares, was to be found "in the place we would have least expected it, in a sign of pain and contradiction, a symbol of torture and death—which against all merely human possibility has become also our token of Christ's victory."[43] Christ "has plundered the house of the ruler of this world, but he did not do it from a safe distance, . . . He did not run away from the fire. He entered into it." Christ's sacrifice, to which the cross at Ground Zero testifies, is for Christian faith the sign of victorious sacrifice against the odds, and the sacrifice that makes the difference.

In this sermon, Rutledge connects the self-giving and sacrifice that occurred on every side amid the horrors of September 11 with the sacrifice of Christ, thus catching up the moving stories of radical self-giving emerging from September 11 into the gospel's decisive pattern of self-giving, resurrection, and God-promised future. Yet, because Rutledge carefully develops this connection within a larger framework, that of God's commitment to redeem the sin-enslaved cosmos, Jesus' death does not get reduced to merely one among many acts of heroism; rather, the pattern of meaning runs in the opposite direction: what may look to us like acts of heroism are, by the grace of God, incorporated into a larger pattern of divine redemption. In this way, the metaphor of sacrifice as unstinting self-donation functions to disclose the ongoing pattern of God's redemptive presence, not only amid the horrors of September 11 and its aftermath, but also amid all the horrors that human beings may experience. Rutledge's sermon frees sacrificial interpretation of Jesus' death from the narrow confines of an individualized transaction that achieves our personal salvation. Rutledge has widened our perspective not only on sacrifice but also on the significance of the cross, locating Jesus' death within the ongoing redemptive work of God to mitigate the power of horrors to overcome us. God's promise made flesh in the risen Christ weighs more heavily than the worst that widespread terrorism can do to cramp and diminish human hope.

As these preachers demonstrate, sacrifice is not a single metaphor but opens up a range of rich possibilities. Sacrifice, understood in many ways as abundant donation and outpouring of life for the sake of generating life, reveals that the death of Jesus is the culmination of his abundantly given life, the outpouring of God's own life that makes us whole.

7

Open Gestures toward Mystery

Cross Talk in Its Liturgical and Cultural Context

During my years as a local church pastor, I took my turn leading an afternoon worship service at a local nursing care facility for older adults. On the whole, preaching was a struggle in that service; a good percentage of those who either made their way, or were delivered, to that service could not follow a sermon. A few were attentive, but others sat staring, unfocused, at the worn green-and-white floor tiles or seemed to be talking to invisible others in the room.

The minute the pianist began playing an old hymn tune, though, everything changed. Heads rose, backs straightened—and the congregation *sang*. A woman who had lost her memory even for the names of her children could sing every word of "The Old Rugged Cross." Later, we would start the Lord's Prayer. A man in the front row, stripped of his capacity for speech by a stroke, would look straight at me, forming every word of the prayer with his lips as best he could.

The oft-repeated words of the prayers we pray and the hymns we sing are the ones that stay with us. A good many of the words we Christians pray and sing in worship are words about Jesus' death and its meaning for us. As much as we preachers may hope that our sermons are a primary shaper of theological imagination for our congregations, we know that the words our congregations pray and sing in worship influence their thinking at least as powerfully, if not even more so.

We preachers need to keep in mind that our sermons take place in a context—the actions, as well as words said and sung, that make up Christian worship. The language our congregants speak, hear, and sing in worship can work alongside our sermons to establish a broad vision of the saving significance of Jesus' death. In this chapter I want to consider how worship can shape a congregation's vision of redemption and suggest ways that preachers and their partners in worship planning can shape worship so that its multiple elements—prayers, liturgical actions, and music, along with the sermon—can bring an array of metaphors into play.

THE DEATH OF JESUS AND THE SACRAMENTS

Right at the center of Christian worship, alongside preaching, are the sacraments of baptism and Holy Communion. Despite the rising and sinking fortunes of various atonement theories through the fluctuations of history and cultures, says liturgical scholar Robert S. Paul, the sacraments have continued to function for Christian worshipers as dramatic interpretive texts in relation to Jesus' death. Jesus himself, Paul points out, did not leave us "any descriptive explanation" of his death; what Jesus *did* do was to institute sacraments that provide a dramatic, enacted, and participatory interpretation of its meaning.[1] The heart of the Christian gospel is that at the cross, God redeems what is God's own. The sacraments are core interpretations of this critical event. When the Lord's Supper and baptism are regularly a part of worship, they powerfully shape believers' understanding of the cross. When the sacraments are neglected, a crucial interpretive text for the meaning of Jesus' life and death is lost.

Participating in the sacraments, Paul reminds us, sets us "in the realm of epic and drama rather than of definition and formula, the realm of worship rather than that of pure theology."[2] Of course, the sacraments are not wordless gesture; word and action interpret one another. In addition, although the sacraments themselves proclaim the gospel, these actions do not stand alone; they need to be accompanied regularly by the preached Word. Moreover, the sacraments are more than dramatic presentations of Jesus' death and its significance; they are participatory. The Lord's Supper and baptism take us up in "a continuing of the mighty acts of God, and especially of his redeeming action in Jesus Christ."[3] In baptism and the Lord's Supper, God's saving word *happens* to us as we are washed and fed. As we participate in the communion meal and baptismal bath, we sense more deeply the import of Jesus' life and death for our lives, for the church, and for the world.

The sacraments insistently hold together Jesus' living and dying. By taking part in baptism and the Lord's Supper, we ourselves become, through water and meal, contemporary flesh-and-blood participants in the outpouring of life that characterizes Jesus' entire career, including his ministry and his death and rising. All that Jesus' death means becomes ours—but all that his life means is "given for us" as well. In the sacraments we "take to ourselves" and for ourselves Christ's God-oriented being in the world. We are baptized into Jesus' dying and rising. Jesus hands over to us at his Table through the actions of breaking and pouring a share in his living and dying, so that the pattern of his life becomes the pattern of ours—life outpoured that brings life.[4]

The most direct and historically stable interpretation of Jesus' death within eucharistic liturgies is found in the Words of Institution. "This is my body, given for you; . . . my blood shed for you." These, the tradition tells us, are the words by which Jesus himself interpreted the meal. The Words of Institution are meant to be said at every celebration of communion in every Christian church, regardless of whether the rest of the words that accompany the meal are supplied by a service book or are composed extemporaneously by the one who presides. The preposition "for" in the Words of Institution is open to multiple interpretations, all of them relevant: "for" in the sense of "representatively," and also in the sense of "for our benefit" and "as gift." We are bidden to eat and drink, so that we are bodily incorporated with the Crucified, and he with us. Christ places himself in our hands at this meal.[5] At the same time, Jesus' body and blood are "for" us in the sense that he hands himself, as well as all of us, body and blood, over to God. Calvin reminds us that we are united by the Spirit with the bodily Christ in heaven.[6] We "remember" Jesus with bodily memory, taking his body and blood into our hands, handing ourselves over to God that Jesus' life may be expressed in us, the church.

THE CROSS IN LITURGIES FOR THE LORD'S SUPPER AND BAPTISM

Liturgies for the Sacrament of the Lord's Supper

The breadth of metaphors found in contemporary eucharistic rites varies considerably from one service book to another. Among contemporary service books, the one that presents the most elaborate array of images and allusions is *The Book of Common Prayer* of the Episcopal Church. In Rite I of *The Book of Common Prayer*, both the standard and alternate versions of the Great Thanksgiving dwell with determined theological focus on sacrifice. The basic prayer states that Jesus made "by his one oblation of himself once offered, a full, perfect, and sufficient sacrifice, oblation, and satisfaction, for the sins of the whole world." His death is meritorious, and we participate in its merits "by faith in his blood." The alternate prayer for Rite I leaves the theological details more open; it states that Jesus suffered death "for our redemption" and "made there a full and perfect sacrifice."[7]

The prayers for Rite II abbreviate (but do not eliminate) the reference to sacrifice, yet add to the sacrifice metaphor themes of Jesus' solidarity with human experience as well as reconciliation between human beings and God: Jesus came "to share our human nature, to live and die as one of us, to reconcile us to . . . the God and Father of all."[8] A robust metaphor of deliverance from captivity and into new life informs Eucharistic Prayer B in Rite II ("In him, you have delivered us from evil; . . . you have brought us out of error into truth, out of sin into righteousness, out of death into life").[9] Reconciliation and healing are the metaphors that interpret Jesus' death in Eucharistic Prayer C, Rite II: "By his blood, he reconciled us. By his wounds, we are healed."[10]

Wisely used, the rites of *The Book of Common Prayer* allow an array of images to shape a congregation's understanding of the significance of Jesus' death for us. The difficulty is that, thanks to local custom or habit, some congregations use only Rite I and therefore hear and speak primarily sacrificial language in connection with Jesus' death. This brings into play the difficulties many theologians cite with overemphasis on sacrifice language unbalanced by other motifs. Altering congregational habit is risky business at best; but it is worth the theological gains if various forms of the eucharistic prayer can be permitted to have their say. Using a variety of language and preaching about the different metaphors used in the prayers—these strategies can introduce breadth and balance.

In the Presbyterian *Book of Common Worship*, the eucharistic prayer for the basic "Service for the Lord's Day" states simply that Jesus' death was "for us," with one of the optional memorial acclamations declaring that Jesus' dying "destroyed our death."[11] Pastors who from time to time use other options for the Great Prayer of Thanksgiving, however, introduce an array of metaphors: deliverance from slavery to sin and death, the overcoming of hostile and hurtful powers, a perfect sacrifice for the sins of the whole world, the demonstration of a love stronger than death, the fulfillment of divine purpose.[12] "Great Thanksgiving G" is remarkable for its multifaceted exploration of what is essentially a ransom or liberation motif. Here, drawing on ancient texts, the prayer declares that Jesus accepts death freely in order "to destroy death, . . . to shatter the chains of the evil one, to trample underfoot the powers of hell, and to lead the righteous into light, to fix the boundaries of death."[13]

The service book of the Christian Church (Disciples of Christ), *Chalice Worship*, employs a range of traditional images including sacrifice, forgiveness, and the giving of life, but emphasizes in particular the freedom with which Jesus gave his life. One prayer is remarkable for the way it takes seriously the full participation of the Trinity at the cross. Explicitly addressing the Triune God, it declares, "*You* . . . gave of *yourself* sacrificially in Christ Jesus" (emphasis added).[14] In addition, Jesus is praised because at the cross he "put an end to death by dying for us" and created a new people. An ecumenical eucharistic prayer in *Chalice Worship* appropriates the language of Philippians 2 to interpret Jesus' death as the self-emptying of Jesus, who takes "the form of a servant."[15]

Most sparse, theologically, among contemporary service books is the *Book of Worship: United Church of Christ*. No allusion to *Jesus' death* as sacrifice appears anywhere here. An invitation to worshipers to present *themselves* as a living sacrifice as they come to the Table is the only sacrifice reference. Most of the prayers simply state that the worshipers "remember" Jesus' death, leaving the event itself virtually uninterpreted beyond a modest statement that it was "for us." One of the five options adds that in his death, Jesus "delivered us from the way of sin and death."[16] An order for use with the sick appropriately recalls that Jesus, who shares our suffering, "accepted the pain of death at the hands of those whom [he] loved."[17]

In contexts where the liturgy of the Lord's Supper is conducted extemporaneously by the presider, pastors have much more liberty to make thoughtful and deliberate use of a wide array of images to interpret the redemptive significance of Jesus' death. Preachers will want to do so with well-balanced attention to the content of the sermon, prayers, and hymns for the service. On occasion, concentrating on a single metaphorical system, especially one that has been neglected in the imagination and worship practices of a particular congregation, may be worthwhile; at other times, two or three images might be deliberately interspersed, keeping the range of imaginative resources broad.

Liturgies for Baptism

Contemporary baptismal liturgies rightly draw parallels not only between baptism and the death of Jesus, but also between Christian baptism and the whole of Jesus' career, including his ministry, his death, and his resurrection. Baptismal liturgies in the contemporary service books of the Christian Church (Disciples of Christ) and United Church of Christ are sparing in their allusions to Jesus' death. The Presbyterian *Book of Common Worship* elaborates the relationship between the death of Jesus and Christian baptism to a much greater degree. In a version of the "Thanksgiving over the Water," Jesus' own death and resurrection is a "baptism" by which we are set free from sin and death, while the baptismal water becomes "a fountain of deliverance" to "wash away sin" (alternative I).[18] Another option speaks of Jesus leading us by his death and resurrection from the bondage of sin into life.[19] An optional canticle at the baptism itself envisions Jesus' passion as having universal cleansing significance, celebrating baptism as "the fountain of life, water made holy by the suffering of Christ, washing all the world."[20]

Preaching on the Sacraments

The profound connections between the death of Jesus and the sacraments are seldom as clear to those who participate in these rites as we may think. How can preachers change this situation? Most congregations need to hear more preaching about the sacraments than they typically do. The metaphors that come into play in sacramental liturgies could be taken up, one by one, in sermons spaced over the course of a year or more. For worship one might choose a variety of liturgies for baptism or communion over successive weeks, months, or liturgical seasons, and then preach about the metaphors of redemption found in these rites. The idea, of course, is not to confuse the congregation with a welter of images, but rather to introduce them to a wealth of metaphors whose implications can be explored.

Pairing the rites with aptly matched biblical texts is important. Preachers can consult the appendix of this book, which indicates which texts of the New Revised Common Lectionary reference the death of Jesus, to coordinate apt texts with various sacramental liturgies.

IMAGES OF REDEMPTION
IN HYMNS AND WORSHIP MUSIC

There are perhaps no words or images that stay with us longer than the ones we sing over and over. A congregation's understanding of the death of Jesus is powerfully shaped by the language of its hymns, praise songs, and prayers. If the music sung in worship brings into view a rich range of images of redemption, it is a gold mine, keeping a congregation's understanding of God's redeeming work rich, open, and lively. On the other hand, if the congregation's musical repertoire offers a narrow range of metaphors and images of redemption, theological imagination in turn will be limited. To keep the fund of metaphors that shape a congregation's theological imagination broad, pastors and those who work alongside them to plan worship need to give close attention to the words that will be sung in every worship service.

Certain classic hymns reflect a broad and deep theological vision of redemption. A fine example is the text of the well-known "Praise, My Soul, the God of Heaven" (an inclusive-language revision of the text, "Praise, My Soul, the King of Heaven") which declares,

> Ransomed, healed, restored, forgiven,
> who, like me, should sing God's praise?[21]

Here, in a single line, no less than four significant dimensions of God's redemptive engagement with us are expressed: We are (1) ransomed (liberated from various captivities), (2) healed (of the sickness of sin and its distortions of human experience), (3) restored (into fellowship with God and one another), and (4) forgiven (released from sin's guilt and alienation, and enabled to extend forgiveness to others, as well).

Many hymn texts, however, imagine redemption in narrower terms. Hymns from the revival service tradition, spanning the mid-eighteenth through early twentieth centuries, often celebrate redemption in highly individualistic language, limiting their vision of salvation to debts settled and heaven assured. One such hymn, "All My Sins Have Been Forgiven," is phrased in the first-person singular throughout. The models of atonement that inform it—penal atonement and sacrifice—are clear:

> My account is closed forever; Jesus Christ has paid it all,
> Shed his blood my sin to cover, paid the price to save my soul.

Although reconciliation receives one passing reference in this hymn, it is undeveloped; a debt-payment motif dominates. The chief reward of salvation celebrated in the hymn is the relief of knowing that "now my soul shall live forever, . . . Thus I journey on to heaven."[22]

That a single model of salvation informs this hymn's vision of redemption is not the problem, in and of itself. There is no reason why a single hymn, like a single sermon, should not explore and celebrate a particular metaphor of redemption. The problem is that in some churches, the *same* handful of models and metaphors inform virtually *every* hymn that mentions Jesus' death. In fact, in the 1974 hymnal *Hymns for the Living Church*, where this hymn appears, the preponderance of hymns focusing on the cross draws on the same two metaphors—penal substitution and sacrifice as blood-covering for sin. Moreover, each one is expressed in the first-person singular, and in no hymn is the church as a body bidden to celebrate redemption and the difference it makes in its shared life. Only occasionally do we find a passing reference to some other metaphor, and then usually within a hymn basically devoted to other themes. Rarely is the celebration of the cross phrased in the first-person *plural* ("we," "our," "us"). Worship leaders in a congregation using this hymnal must look elsewhere to find worship music that envisions the saving significance of Jesus' death for estranged social groups or for a world of hostility and violence.

In contrast, the Presbyterian hymnal, published twenty years later, includes only a handful of hymns that dwell exclusively on the death of Jesus. In those that do, allusions to penal substitution are virtually absent. Where sacrifice motifs appear, they are blended with many other metaphors and motifs. The 1964 Methodist hymnal occupies something of a middle ground. Certainly the cross figured strongly in the hymns of Charles Wesley, but while sacrifice and substitution are recurrent motifs, Wesley's creative theological vision ensured that worshipers would be offered texts rich with varied metaphors of redemption.

On the whole, newer hymn texts use more varied ideas and images in connection with Jesus' death than older ones do; they draw a richer diversity of metaphors into relationship with Jesus' death. Using newer hymns that do not appear in the congregation's standard hymnal will require printing permission, but it is well worth the effort. For example, a Lenten text by James Gertmenian, "Throughout These Lenten Days and Nights," refers to Jesus as "the Lamb of God, who found in weakness greater power," and as "one who wore for us the crown of thorns and slept in death that we might wake to life." Gertmenian aligns the Lenten journey with the journey of Christ to the cross and beyond. Suffering is not celebrated here in and of itself, nor is the focus on our own "crosses to bear"; rather, our suffering is with and for a suffering world: "We bear the silence, cross and pain of human burdens, human strife." We are indeed called by the Spirit "through Calvary's dying, dark and deep"—but on toward Easter and the fullness of God's reign.[23]

Another striking text, translated from the original Hungarian by Erik Routley, is "There in God's Garden." Jesus and the cross on which he dies are juxtaposed here, envisioned as a suffering tree whose limbs embrace the nations and whose foliage heals, despite the scars the tree suffers. Human greed and indifference cannot destroy its life or its life-giving capacity. We foresee our own death and resurrection through that of Jesus, and envision God's future for us all in a haunting final stanza.[24]

Music produced by contemporary Christian performers and publishers has become a major imagination-shaping influence in the faith and practice of many North American Christians today. The number of congregations that sing music primarily from these sources is growing. Much contemporary worship music exhibits an individualistic soteriology, drawing mainly on sacrifice and penal substitution motifs. In recent years, however, some contemporary Christian artists have begun to produce lyrics that point more boldly to the social and ethical dimensions of redemption. This suggests a gradual but perceptible widening of theological vision in this music tradition.

Also encouraging is the influence of "emergent church" leaders who are expressing concern about rampantly "me"-centered theology and worship in too many self-avowed evangelical communities. "Emergent church" leaders are reclaiming the sacraments, stressing the corporate nature of Christian life, and strengthening the connection between spirituality and ethics.[25] These are heartening developments, suggesting that congregations and their leaders are looking for worship that paints a broad picture of God's redemptive action in the world.

Choosing Music for Worship

The point is that the texts people sing matter. Because words set to music are more memorable than spoken words, they shape how believers envision the world, God, redemption, and justice. Preachers concerned to make sure that worship music is helpful, not limiting, to congregational imagination can do three things. First, they and their partners in worship planning and leadership can begin by paying close attention to what is being sung in worship. What is being said about redemption? Is salvation all about the individual? Are some metaphors stressed far more than others? Just as importantly, what is *not* being said? Do worship songs and hymns speak of God's will to deliver the cosmos from its bondage to suffering and death? Do they envision God's opposition to social sins—greed, prejudice, the abuse of power?

Second, worship leaders can encourage diversity in musical texts in every worship service, whether the style is classic, contemporary, or a blend. Where the availability of sufficiently broad texts is a problem (either because the congregation is committed to a particular hymnal for worship that provides limited choices, or contemporary worship resources work with a limited range of metaphors), it will be well worth the effort and expense to find new and different hymns. Worship leaders need to invest in an up-to-date library of new hymnals from a variety of denominations, even if their congregations are not ready to invest in new hymnals for weekly worship. Often, licensing permission for one-time printing of a hymn text is granted without financial charge; but a line in the church budget to cover occasional licensing fees is a good idea.

Third, worship leaders can consider pairing classic texts with updated tunes. Say, for example, that a classic hymn text offers wonderfully rich language for redemption, but it is paired in the hymnal with a tune not at all suited to the congregation's customary piano-and-percussion style of music. Worship leaders can consult the metrical indices of tunes (found in the back pages of every standard hymnal) to find a different tune that is a good match, metrically, with the hymn text but lends itself better to the instrumentation the congregation prefers. The only caution here is to make sure that the points of emphasis in the chosen new tune fit the text, and that the mood of the music is suited to the text's meaning.

Interpreting the Cross Talk We Sing

Worshipers enjoy learning about the texts in their hymnals. They welcome open, informal forums where youth and adults together can reflect openly and thoughtfully about the images of redemption they speak and sing in worship.

Not long ago I led an adult education forum at an Episcopal church on what Christians believe about the difference Jesus' death makes. I brought a stack of hymn texts (downloaded from the Web) as well as a supply of the congregation's hymnals.[26] After a short presentation on the metaphorical character of our cross talk, I invited the group to discover with me the metaphors in the hymns before us. Together we explored how hymns interpreted the death of Jesus, paying attention to the eras in which they were written.

To my surprise, although many in the room were lifelong Episcopalians, many recognized a number of texts I had brought that represented the "blood hymns" of the nineteenth to early twentieth-century evangelical tradition ("Power in the Blood," "There Is a Fountain Filled with Blood," "Are You Washed in the Blood?" "What Can Wash Away My Sin?" and so on). While none of these were in their standard hymnal, they had picked them up at summer camp meetings or as children, visiting other churches with relatives. We talked about what they found either helpful or troubling about these "blood hymns." We also considered the allusions to Jesus' death and its meaning in the seasonal hymns of Holy Week. We found that certain metaphors of redemption were very common, and others merited only a reference here and there.

More than one woman in the room expressed misgivings about connections in hymns and liturgies, explicit or implied, between Jesus' suffering and the kinds of behaviors enjoined in particular and disproportionately upon women in many societies—doing without, working themselves "to death" for others, enduring verbal and physical abuse without complaint as "good witnesses" to Christian faith. For some, it was the first time they had felt free to raise these questions in a church context.

Conversations like this can help church members notice the distinctive claims of the different metaphors at work in the texts they are singing, allow them to air their concerns, and explore fresh ways to consider the meaning of Jesus' death for their worship and witness.

Preaching Notes

The cup that is "the blood of Christ, shed for us," is announced at nearly every communion liturgy. Innumerable hymns in evangelical traditions celebrate the blood of Jesus as that which washes away sin. Few symbols associated with the cross can equal the symbol of shed blood in inspiring either adoration or revulsion among Christians. Two sermons, one by Angela M. Edwards in the African American preaching tradition, the

other by Episcopal preacher Barbara Brown Taylor, forthrightly confront the blood of Jesus that the Lord's Supper places at the center of the
dramatic, sacramental enactment of the gospel.

Sermons that take for their theme the phrase "sprinkle this blood" are a
part of the repertoire of many African American preachers. Biblical allusions in a sermon on this topic are typically the murder of Abel by his
brother Cain coupled with Hebrews 12:24, which says that the shed
blood of Christ "speaks a better word than the blood of Abel." Different preachers take up the theme of the sprinkled blood that "speaks" and
creatively adapt it for a specific congregation and occasion, much the
way a jazz musician might improvise on a familiar tune.

Edwards's sermon "Sprinkle This Blood" belongs to this tradition.[27]
Beginning with the first story of murder in the Bible, Edwards points
out that Abel's blood was said to cry out to God from the ground. Genesis 4 teaches us that "blood can speak." We recoil at the sight of blood,
Edwards observes—but maybe it is not just that blood suggests wound-
ing and pain, or that it confronts us with our own mortal vulnerability.
"Could it be because we know [that] blood speaks? Could it be [that]
we are afraid to listen, to hear? Could the blood cry out from the contradiction, conflict and inconsistency of blood being on the ground
when blood is to be in the body and give life?" asks Edwards.[28] Moreover, says Edwards, "It is clear that not only does blood speak, it [also]
has God as a divine audience. . . . The blood speaks truth, speaks of the
history of pain, abuse, inflicted suffering" that cries out for redress.[29]

Edwards turns our attention to the speaking blood of "three broth-
ers," Abel, Martin Luther King Jr., and Jesus. Their shed blood speaks,
as blood always speaks, and it convicts. Yet while the shed blood of Abel
or of King "cries out for justice and retribution, the precious blood of
Jesus cries out for forgiveness and reconciliation." Edwards begins a
chantlike litany of New Testament texts that announce the "better
word," the word that not only calls for justice but also accomplishes it,
"spoken" by Jesus' blood: "There is a new covenant based upon the
blood that speaks a better word. . . . So, sprinkle this blood!" There is
freedom and redemption, peace and forgiveness, justification and new
life in this blood, "so sprinkle this blood!" In the places of shame and
guilt in personal or family life, in community conflict or global strife,
the blood of Jesus "speaks a better word. . . . So sprinkle this blood."[30]

As the sermon rises to its closing crescendo, Edwards skillfully rings
the changes on familiar themes in connection with the symbol of the

"blood of Jesus," but deepens and expands the symbolism to press home a message about social justice and social change.

A more specifically sacramental focus shapes a sermon by Barbara Brown Taylor, "Blood Covenant." Taylor begins with a description of the sorts of blood pacts that human beings make—everything from the pledges of eternal devotion that children make as they rub their pricked fingertips together, to deadly serious pledges of fidelity to death still practiced in some cultures around the world, involving slashed flesh and bloody meals.[31]

Blood matters, says Taylor, and blood makes connections. In the blood sacrifices of the Old Testament, it was believed that life was in the blood. Life "outlived its temporary host, and it was the shedding of blood that mattered, . . . the offering of it," not the death of the sacrificed animal in itself.[32] If we imagine that blood and its power to make connections does not really matter, then, suggests Taylor, perhaps we have not been paying close enough attention at the communion rail. If we do not, children certainly do, however. Taylor tells the story of a girl of about six who was indeed paying very close attention as Taylor moved along the rail, offering the cup. When she came to the little girl with the words "This is my blood," she jerked away in horror and declared: "I don't want any!" The cup, says Taylor, is just what the child took it to be: a covenant in blood, a pact that cost blood.[33] Jesus makes his lifeblood our life. He gives us the cup, knowing as he does so that "we will not be innocent of the blood in this cup." We would do—have done—no better than the disciples to whom Jesus first offered the cup, the ones who "turn him in [and] scatter to the four winds at the first sign of trouble."[34]

Taylor stresses that the point of the blood is life, not death—the life in the cup, not the death. "It is the life that is being offered, the life that rushes out of the cup like a spring of living water." In the cup, God makes God's own self to be blood kin to us. It is the ultimate self-offering, God's complete self-giving to us. Our part is to accept the cup and drink the life freely given in it.[35]

These sermons by Edwards and Taylor confront what for many twenty-first-century Christians is least comfortable about the cross: the shedding of blood. Yet in the skilled hands of these preachers, the blood becomes testimony to God's justice and the gift of the very life of God for the world.

Reaching for Cultural Relevance:
Can We Construct New Metaphors?

A question we have not touched on so far is whether or not it is appropriate and useful for preachers to create *new* metaphors to connect with Jesus' death. Are biblical metaphors the only reliable metaphors, or is it both necessary and appropriate to find altogether new ways of "imagining" redemption? If new metaphors are permissible, what safeguards should a preacher consider to check the resonance of the metaphor with the whole history of Christian reflection on the cross?

Some theologians insist that particular metaphors should be privileged in our interpretations of redemption. For example, theologian Hans Boersma argues that some metaphors function in theological reflection as "root metaphors." Certain of the tradition's metaphors deserve, says Boersma, to become "models" of the sort that Sallie McFague and others describe. Boersma posits four criteria for such "root metaphors" or models: (1) the metaphor has proved to be durably resonant with Christian tradition over time; (2) it discloses deeper understanding of redemption with "logical consistency"; (3) it displays "ability to enable our imagination and creativity to flourish"; and (4) as the metaphor is used, its limitations are acknowledged. No metaphor will have the same resonance and relevance for all persons and all situations.[36]

These criteria are helpful. Certain metaphors have proved to be more widely useful and enduring in Christian interpretation than others. At the same time, historically speaking, some of the models we regard as most weighty today were innovative in their time. Arguably, Anselm's satisfaction metaphor for atonement, drawn from the social norms and dynamics of the feudal, honor-based society of his time, was a fresh lens through which to "imagine" redemption. Similarly, although John Calvin drew on Pauline language about law for his elaboration of a penal understanding of atonement, his interpretation shows that he was much influenced by the assumptions and norms of sixteenth-century jurisprudence. Similarly, while James Cone's metaphor of the lynching tree, discussed in chapter 4, has obvious affinities with the "tree" on which Jesus was killed, it is a thoroughly contemporary nineteenth- and twentieth-century symbol that connects the cross with the history of slavery and racism as these have been experienced in North America.

The question may not be so much whether we can bring new metaphorical resources to bear on our interpretation of the cross, but how to do so. Rather than discuss these matters in the abstract, it may be more useful to examine a recent project that tries to do just this. Main-taining that virtually *every* traditional metaphor of redemption has either produced unacceptable doctrinal effects for women and minorities, or has failed to guide ongoing, transformative praxis for the church, L. Susan Bond proposes that we reinterpret the saving significance of Jesus' death through a metaphor of "salvage." Throughout Jesus' life, but especially and most pointedly at the cross, God salvages creation, getting God's hands dirty, so to speak, as God rescues from the wreckage of human sin and evil not only the human future but also all creation. The metaphor of redemption as a divine salvage operation, Bond argues, brings a gritty reality to God's active commitment to radically transform, at great cost to God's own self, what is broken, damaged, soiled, and deemed by many only fit for the rubbish heap. The God revealed in Christ is "one who will risk everything to salvage the death-bent world."[37]

Salvage, Bond argues, meets a list of criteria to test the theological and rhetorical-contextual plausibility of a proposed redemption metaphor.[38] A new metaphor, says Bond, needs to fit plausibly with the authoritative texts, ongoing history, and contemporary liturgical practices of the church, and at the same time, project useful paradigms for transforma-tive witness on the part of the church today. Furthermore, a usable metaphor will maintain the priority of God in redemption, "fit" the his-torical data about the life and ministry of Jesus, make solid connections with the problems of sin and suffering (without valorizing suffering), and prove salutary, not damaging, for women and society's most vulnerable.[39]

The salvage metaphor has biblical plausibility. First Corinthians 1:26–31 suggests points of connection: "God chose what is low and despised in the world, things that are not, to reduce to nothing things that are" (v. 28). Salvage suggests that God identifies with and reclaims what the world counts as refuse, bearing witness to a power that "looks weak to those who regularly practice domination."[40] God's determina-tion to be among society's most vulnerable, raising up the fallen and despised, is well attested throughout Scripture. Mary's Magnificat (Luke 1:46–55) comes immediately to mind.

Like the more traditional "salvation," Bond's "salvage" metaphor is rooted in the Latin, *salvare*. "The metaphor of salvage," writes Bond, "has the same linguistic source as salvation but offers a more immedi-ate physical image." An advantage of salvage over more traditional metaphors, in Bond's view, is that the metaphor of salvage "allows us to bracket out ontological differences and traditional explanations." By this Bond means, among other things, that "salvage" allows for a Christology of the kind she herself embraces, one that regards Jesus Christ as merely human and in no sense divine, yet does not require such a view.[41] One need not share either Bond's reluctance to claim for Jesus a unique relationship to God (or for that matter, her despairing conclusions about the positive potential in traditional metaphors) to entertain the possibility of using a new metaphor such as "salvage."

Wisely noting that "metaphors cannot be pressed too literally into service," Bond tests both the capacities and limits of the salvage metaphor. Salvage can be related meaningfully to individual sin, and at the same time it can disclose how God addresses sin on a social level, including the way humans use political power to the advantage of some while diminishing others.[42] Salvage meets Bond's criterion of providing paradigms for ongoing social praxis in continuity with God's work of redemption: this metaphor is strong precisely where too many soteriological metaphors can appear weak, making clear the ethical practices that God's way of redeeming the world requires of the redeemed community. "Salvage requires us to touch what the world has seen fit to throw away," says Bond.[43] It is easy to envision connections to the work of the church, especially in its ministries of care and social change.

What does the metaphor of salvage disclose, specifically, about Jesus' death? Bond may underplay the limitations of the salvage metaphor as it relates to the cross, specifically. Bond does not make it entirely clear how Jesus' death, in particular, is integral to God's salvage operation. Although Bond declares that "the cross and resurrection disclose God's presence to those who suffer, [and disclose] God's alternative to abusive power, and the transformative hope of renewed life," Bond does not make it entirely clear who is doing the "salvaging" at the cross, or what is being salvaged there.[44] Bond's metaphor may help us more to discover the way the dynamics of redemption are ongoing, requiring our participation, than in illuminating Jesus' death in itself. Yet we can recognize in the cross God's bodily and vulnerable identification with what the world discards. We can also recognize that the cross is the price for unswervingly pursuing God's salvaging purpose. Still, the salvage metaphor may need to be accompanied by others to help us see clearly why this particular death stands at the very center of God's redemptive work.

Certainly Bond's salvage metaphor is intriguing. It bears obvious relevance for a consumption-crazed age, although preachers need to supplement it in their preaching with other images. Bond is to be commended for her daring foray into a fresh vision of redemption. As human experiences of sin and suffering, violence and estrangement take on new forms through time, we may need fresh metaphors to disclose the relevance of God's redeeming work to these realities. No metaphor or model has ever been sufficient to disclose fully the meaning of Jesus' death in answer to every historical epoch, every culture, every dilemma; but throughout the history of Christian reflection on the death of Jesus, theologians have creatively used the imaginative resources of their times to illuminate the redemptive significance of the cross.

Leanne Van Dyk writes of the cross, "There was some kind of victory that took place, some kind of power shift in the universe, some kind of ransom paid, some kind of healing initiated, some ultimate kind of love displayed, some kind of dramatic rescue effected." Yet "the terrible paradox of the Christian faith is that this rescue, this victory, this healing happened because of a death—a notorious public execution. This is the dark mystery of the atonement."[45]

Preachers have no choice but to speak of this "dark mystery." We step into pulpits in prosperous churches or impoverished ones, amid rolling green landscapes, bustling commercial districts, or urban decay. We face congregations bonded to one another in love, riven by grief, or locked in bitter conflict. No matter the setting or situation, the preacher's task is to help those who face them from the pews to "imagine" redemption, then and there. Cross talk is daring and necessary speech that, through the open-ended, is-and-is-not gesture of metaphor, imagines the dynamics of redemption in the concrete places where people sin and suffer, struggle and hope. We declare that God's promise is kept and being kept in the One whose life is continually poured out to give life to the world, the One who calls us into God's future by way of his cross.

Biblical Texts Referencing the Death of Jesus
New Revised Common Lectionary

Lectionary Reading	Passion Accounts	Gospel Allusions to Passion	OT Allusions	Other NT Material	Related
Year A					
1st Sunday of Advent					
2nd Sunday of Advent					
3rd Sunday of Advent					
4th Sunday of Advent				Titus 2:11–14, esp. v. 14	
Nativity of the Lord Proper 1					
Nativity of the Lord Proper 2					
Nativity of the Lord Proper 3					
1st Sunday after Christmas Day				Heb. 2:10–18, esp. vv. 17–18	
Holy Name of Jesus				Phil. 2:5–11	
New Year's Day					
Epiphany of the Lord					
Baptism of the Lord				Acts 10:34–43, esp. v. 39	
2nd Sunday after the Epiphany		John 1:29–42, esp. v. 29	Isa. 49:1–7, esp. v. 7		
3rd Sunday after the Epiphany				1 Cor. 1:10–18, esp. v. 18	
4th Sunday after the Epiphany				1 Cor. 1:18–31, esp. v. 23	
Transfiguration Sunday					
Ash Wednesday				2 Cor. 5:20b–6:10, esp. v. 21	
1st Sunday in Lent				Rom. 5:12–19	
2nd Sunday in Lent				John 3:1–17, esp. v. 14	
3rd Sunday in Lent				Rom. 5:1–11	
4th Sunday in Lent					
5th Sunday in Lent					
Liturgy of the Palms					
Liturgy of the Passion	Matt. 26:14–27:66 Matt. 27:11–54		Isa. 50:4–9a Ps. 31:9–16	Phil. 2:5–11	
Monday of Holy Week		John 12:1–11	Isa. 42:1–9 Ps. 36:5–11	Heb. 9:11–15	
Tuesday of Holy Week		John 12:20–36	Isa. 49:1–7	1 Cor. 1:18–31	
Wednesday of Holy Week		John 13:21–32	Isa. 50:4–9a	Heb. 12:1–3	
Maundy Thursday		John 13:1–17, 31b–35	Exod. 12:1–4, (5–10), 11–14	1 Cor. 11:23–26	
Good Friday	John 18:1–19:42		Isa. 52:13–53:12 Ps. 22	Heb. 10:16–25 Heb. 4:14–16; 5:7–9	
Holy Saturday	Matt. 27:57–66 John 19:38–42		Job 14:1–4 Lam. 3:1–9, 19–24		

Biblical Texts Referencing the Death of Jesus; New Revised Common Lectionary, Year A.

Lectionary Reading	Passion Accounts	Gospel Allusions to Passion	OT Allusions	Other NT Material	Related
Year A					
Easter Day				Acts 10:34–43	
2nd Sunday of Easter				Acts 2:14a, 22–32	
3rd Sunday of Easter		Luke 24:13–35		1 Pet. 1:17–23	
4th Sunday of Easter				1 Pet. 2:19–25	
5th Sunday of Easter		John 14:1–14	Ps. 31:1–5, 15–16, esp. v. 5		
6th Sunday of Easter		John 14:15–21		1 Pet. 3:13–22	
Ascension Sunday					
Day of Pentecost					
Trinity Sunday					
Proper 4				Rom. 1:16–17; 3:22b–28, (29–31), esp. 3:25	
Proper 5				Rom. 4:13–25, esp. v. 25	
Proper 6				Rom. 5:1–8	
Proper 7			Ps. 69:7–10, (11–15), 16–18	Rom. 6:1b–11	
Proper 8			Gen. 22:1–14		
Proper 9			Zech. 9:9–12		
Proper 10				Rom. 8:1–11	
Proper 11					
Proper 12				Rom. 8:26–39, esp. v. 32	
Proper 13					
Proper 14					
Proper 15					
Proper 16					
Proper 17		Matt. 16:21–28			
Proper 18			Exod. 12:1–14		
Proper 19				Rom. 14:1–12, esp. v. 9	
Proper 20					
Proper 21				Phil. 2:1–13	
Proper 22		Matt. 21:33–46			Phil. 3:4b–14
Proper 23					
Proper 24					
Proper 25					
Proper 26					
All Saints Day				Rev. 7:9–17, esp. v. 14	
Proper 28					
Proper 29					
Christ the King					

Biblical Texts Referencing the Death of Jesus; New Revised Common Lectionary, Year B.

Lectionary Reading	Passion Accounts	Gospel Allusions to Passion	OT Allusions	Other NT Material	Related
Year B					
1st Sunday of Advent	*				
2nd Sunday of Advent					
3rd Sunday of Advent					
4th Sunday of Advent					
Nativity of the Lord Proper 1				Titus 2:11–14	
Nativity of the Lord Proper 2					
Nativity of the Lord Proper 3					
1st Sunday after Christmas Day		Luke 2:22–40, esp. 34–35			
Holy Name of Jesus				Phil. 2:5–13	
New Year's Day					
Epiphany of the Lord					Ps. 72:1–7, 10–14, esp. v. 14
Baptism of the Lord					
2nd Sunday after the Epiphany					
3rd Sunday after the Epiphany					
4th Sunday after the Epiphany					
5th Sunday after the Epiphany					
6th Sunday after the Epiphany					1 Cor. 8:1–13, esp. v. 11
7th Sunday after the Epiphany					
Transfiguration Sunday					
Ash Wednesday					
1st Sunday in Lent				1 Pet. 3:18–22	
2nd Sunday in Lent		Mark 8:31–38			Ps. 22:23–31
3rd Sunday in Lent		John 2:13–22		1 Cor. 1:18–25	
4th Sunday in Lent		John 3:14–21	Num. 21:4–9		
5th Sunday in Lent		John 12:20–33		Heb. 5:5–10	
Liturgy of the Palms					
Liturgy of the Passion	Matt. 27:57–66		Isa. 50:4–9a	Phil. 2:5–11	
Monday of Holy Week		John 12:1–11	Isa. 42:1–9 Ps. 36:5–11	Heb. 9:11–15	
Tuesday of Holy Week		John 12:20–36	Isa. 49:1–7	1 Cor. 1:18–31	
Wednesday of Holy Week		John 13:21–32	Isa. 50:4–9a	Heb. 12:1–3	
Maundy Thursday		John 13:1–17, 31b–35	Exod. 12:1–4, (5–10), 11–14	1 Cor. 11:23–26	
Good Friday	John 18:1–19:42		Isa. 52:13–53:12 Ps. 22	Heb. 10:16–25 Heb. 4:14–16; 5:7–9	
Holy Saturday	Matt. 27:57–66 John 19:38–42		Job 14:1–14 Lam. 3:1–9, 19–24		
Easter Day				Acts 10:34–43 1 Cor. 15:1–11	
2nd Sunday of Easter					
3rd Sunday of Easter					

Biblical Texts Referencing the Death of Jesus; New Revised Common Lectionary, Year B.

Lectionary Reading	Passion Accounts	Gospel Allusions to Passion	OT Allusions	Other NT Material	Related
Year B					
4th Sunday of Easter					
5th Sunday of Easter					
6th Sunday of Easter					
Ascension Sunday		Luke 24:44–53			
Day of Pentecost					
Trinity Sunday		John 3:1–17			
Proper 4					
Proper 5					
Proper 6					
Proper 7					
Proper 8					
Proper 9					
Proper 10					
Proper 11				Eph. 2:11–22	Ps. 89:20–37
Proper 12					
Proper 13					
Proper 14					John 6:35, 41–51
Proper 15					John 6:51–58
Proper 16					
Proper 17					
Proper 18					
Proper 19		Mark 8:27–38			
Proper 20		Mark 9:30–37			
Proper 21					
Proper 22					
Proper 23			Ps. 22:1–15		
Proper 24		Mark 10:35–45	Is. 53:4–12	Heb. 5:1–10	
Proper 25				Heb. 7:23–28	
Proper 26				Heb. 9:11–14	
All Saints Day				Heb. 9:24–28	
Proper 28				Heb. 10:11–14, (15–18), 19–25	
Proper 29					Rev. 1:4b–9
Christ the King			1 Tim. 2:1–7		

Biblical Texts Referencing the Death of Jesus; New Revised Common Lectionary, Year C.

Lectionary Reading	Passion Accounts	Gospel Allusions to Passion	OT Allusions	Other NT Material	Related
Year C					
1st Sunday of Advent					
2nd Sunday of Advent					
3rd Sunday of Advent					
4th Sunday of Advent					Heb. 10:5–10
Nativity of the Lord Proper 1				Titus 2:11–14	
Nativity of the Lord Proper 2					

Biblical Texts Referencing the Death of Jesus; New Revised Common Lectionary, Year C.

Lectionary Reading	Passion Accounts	Gospel Allusions to Passion	OT Allusions	Other NT Material	Related
Year C					
Nativity of the Lord Proper 3					
1st Sunday after Christmas Day					
Holy Name of Jesus					
New Year's Day					
Epiphany of the Lord					
Baptism of the Lord					
2nd Sunday after the Epiphany					
3rd Sunday after the Epiphany					
4th Sunday after the Epiphany					
5th Sunday after the Epiphany				1 Cor. 15:1–11	
6th Sunday after the Epiphany					1 Cor. 15:12–20
Transfiguration Sunday					
Ash Wednesday					
1st Sunday in Lent					
2nd Sunday in Lent					Luke 13:31–35
3rd Sunday in Lent					
4th Sunday in Lent					
5th Sunday in Lent		John 12:1–8			
Liturgy of the Palms					
Liturgy of the Passion	Matt. 27:57–66, or John 19:38–42		Isa. 50:4–9a Ps. 31:9–16	Phil. 2:5–11	
Monday of Holy Week		John 12:1–11	Isa. 42:1–9 Ps. 36:5–11	Heb. 9:11–15	
Tuesday of Holy Week		John 12:20–36	Isa. 49:1–7	1 Cor. 1:18–31	
Wednesday of Holy Week		John 13:21–32	Isa. 50:4–9a	Heb. 12:1–3	
Maundy Thursday		John 13:1–17, 31b–35	Exod. 12:1–4, (5–10), 11–14	1 Cor. 11:23–26	
Good Friday	John 18:1–19:42		Isa. 52:13–53:12 Ps. 22	Heb. 10:16–25 Heb. 4:14–16; 5:7–9	
Holy Saturday	Matt. 27:57–66 John 19:38–42		Job 14:1–14 Lam. 3:1–9, 19–24		
Easter Day				Acts 10:34–43	
2nd Sunday of Easter		John 20:19–31		Acts 5:27–31	Rev. 1:4–8
3rd Sunday of Easter				Rev. 5:11–14	
4th Sunday of Easter					
5th Sunday of Easter					
6th Sunday of Easter					
Ascension Sunday		Luke 24:44–53			
Day of Pentecost					
Trinity Sunday					
Proper 4					
Proper 5					
Proper 6				Gal. 2:15–21	
Proper 7					
Proper 8					

Biblical Texts Referencing the Death of Jesus; New Revised Common Lectionary, Year C.

Lectionary Reading	Passion Accounts	Gospel Allusions to Passion	OT Allusions	Other NT Material	Related
Year C					
Proper 9					
Proper 10					
Proper 11					
Proper 12				Col. 2:6–15, (16–19)	
Proper 13					
Proper 14					
Proper 15					
Proper 16					Heb. 12:18–29
Proper 17					
Proper 18					
Proper 19					
Proper 20				1 Tim. 2:1–7	
Proper 21					
Proper 22					
Proper 23					
Proper 24					
Proper 25					
Proper 26					
All Saints Day					
Proper 28					
Proper 29	Luke 23:33–43				
Christ the King					

Notes

Introduction

1. See, for example, such recent works as: Anthony Bartlett, *Cross Purposes: The Violent Grammar of Christian Atonement* (Harrisburg: Trinity Press International, 2001); Mark D. Baker and Joel B. Green, *Recovering the Scandal of the Cross: Atonement in New Testament and Contemporary Contexts* (Grand Rapids: Baker Academic, 2006); Simon Barrow and Jonathan Bartley, eds., *Consuming Passion: Why the Killing of Jesus Really Matters* (London: Darton, Longman & Todd, 2005); Han Boersma, *Violence, Hospitality, and the Cross: Reappropriating the Atonement Tradition* (Grand Rapids: Baker Academic, 2004); L. Susan Bond, *Trouble with Jesus: Women, Christology, and Preaching* (St. Louis: Chalice Press, 1999); Rita Nakashima Brock and Rebecca Ann Parker, *Proverbs of Ashes: Violence, Redemptive Suffering, and the Search for What Saves Us* (Boston: Beacon Press, 2001); Alberto L. García and A. R. Victor Raj, eds., *The Theology of the Cross for the Twenty-first Century* (St. Louis: Concordia Publishing, 2002); Douglas John Hall, *The Cross in Our Context: Jesus and the Suffering World* (Minneapolis: Augsburg Fortress Press, 2003); S. Mark Heim, *Saved from Sacrifice: A Theology of the Cross* (Grand Rapids: Eerdmans, 2006); Darby Kathleen Ray, *Deceiving the Devil: Atonement, Abuse, and Ransom* (Cleveland: Pilgrim Press, 1998); Peter Schmiechen, *Saving Power: Theories of Atonement and Forms of the Church* (Grand Rapids: Eerdmans, 2005); JoAnne Marie Terrell, *Power in the Blood? The Cross in African-American Experience* (Maryknoll: Orbis Books, 1998); Marit Trelstad, ed., *Cross Examinations: Readings on the Meaning of the Cross Today* (Minneapolis: Augsburg Fortress, 2006); and J. Denny Weaver, *Nonviolent Atonement* (Grand Rapids: Eerdmans, 2001).

2. There are exceptions, of course. See, for example, the theologically thoughtful Passion Sunday and Holy Week sermons of Fleming Rutledge in *The Undoing of Death: Sermons for Holy Week and Easter* (Grand Rapids: Eerdmans, 2002) and the Good Friday sermons in the brief collection by Kenneth Leech, *We Preach Christ Crucified: The Proclamation of the Cross in a Dark Age* (Boston: Cowley Publications, 1994).

3. Martin Luther, *Luther's Works*, edited by Jaroslav Pelikan and Helmut T. Pelikan, vol. 31 (St. Louis: Concordia Publishing and Fortress Press, 1955–), 41.

4. The phrase "key signature" in relation to the cross and Christian faith is from

Jürgen Moltmann, *The Crucified God: The Cross of Christ as the Foundation and Criticism of Theology*, trans. R. A. Wilson and John Bowden (New York: Harper & Row, 1974), 3.

5. Similar phrasing has been adopted by Baker and Green, *Recovering the Scandal of the Cross*.

6. See Fernando F. Segovia and Mary Ann Tolbert, eds., *Reading from This Place*, vol. 1, *Social Location and Biblical Interpretation in the United States* (Minneapolis: Fortress, 1995); and idem, vol. 2, *Social Location and Biblical Interpretation in Global Perspective* (Minneapolis: Fortress, 2000); and also Brian K. Blount, *Can I Get a Witness? Reading Revelation through African American Culture* (Louisville: Westminster John Knox Press, 2005).

7. See Segovia, "'And They Began to Speak in Other Tongues': Competing Modes of Discourse in Contemporary Biblical Criticism," in Segovia and Tolbert, *Reading from This Place*, 1:28–29, 32; and Fernando F. Segovia, "Cultural Studies and Contemporary Biblical Criticism: Ideological Criticism as Mode of Discourse," in Segovia and Tolbert, *Reading from This Place*, 2:10–17; and see also Blount, *Can I Get a Witness? Reading Revelation through African American Culture*, 12–26.

8. David H. Kelsey, *Imagining Redemption* (Louisville: Westminster John Knox Press, 2005), 43.

9. Schmiechen, *Saving Power*, 4–6.

10. Christian preaching, James F. Kay reminds us, performs what it says: preachers' proclamation that we are "in Christ" enacts and effects God's promise to make all things new. Kay, "The Word of the Cross at the Turn of the Ages," *Interpretation* 53, no. 1 (January 1999): 44–56.

1. At a Loss for Words

1. David Van Biema, "Why Did Jesus Die?" *Time* 163, no. 15 (April 12, 2004): 54–61.

2. Ibid., 61.

3. Gustav Aulén, *Christus Victor: An Historical Study of the Three Main Types of the Idea of Atonement* (London: SPCK, 1931).

4. Arguably, another view that might well claim the "classic" designation is a participation, or *theōsis*, view of atonement, discernible in Paul and widely embraced in the Eastern church.

5. For a historical examination of the parallel development of a retributive understanding of criminal justice and penal versions of atonement theory, see Timothy Gorringe, *God's Just Vengeance: Crime, Violence, and the Rhetoric of Salvation* (Cambridge: Cambridge University Press, 1996).

6. Shirley Guthrie separates the "classic" view into two similar, but distinct images—one a marketplace image in which a ransom is paid for slaves; the other, a military image in which captives are freed. See Guthrie, *Christian Doctrine*, rev.

ed. (Louisville: Westminster John Knox Press, 1994), 252–53. Alister McGrath treats the paradigm of sacrifice as a separate, enduring interpretation of the cross, alongside *Christus Victor*, Anselmian satisfaction, and moral-exemplar theories. See *Christian Theology: An Introduction*, 3rd ed. (Oxford: Blackwell Publishers, 2001), 411–30.

7. Nancy J. Duff, "Atonement and the Christian Life: Reformed Doctrine from a Feminist Perspective," *Interpretation* 53, no. 1 (January 1999): 23.

8. Schmiechen, *Saving Power*. Schmiechen discusses sacrifice, justification by grace, penal substitution, liberation, the renewal of creation, the restoration of the creation ("satisfaction"), Christ as goal of creation, and three versions of reconciliation: Christ as mediator of true knowledge of God, as reconciler, and as revealer of wondrous love.

9. African American, feminist, womanist, and postcolonialist theologians share other methodological commitments as well. A basic methodological principle is that theology is never an abstract, purely "rational" enterprise; it is always a discourse undertaken out of a set of vested interests. In other words, although a theologian may claim to derive one's own theology strictly from the official texts of the Christian tradition, other factors shape that theologian's assumptions and visions, including where one stands with respect to ecclesiastical or academic power, social privilege, economic status, gender, and other parameters. The principle of doctrinal effect is actually derivative from a more-overarching principle, that theology must be done with close attention to the concrete, the particular, and the specific. Sweeping generalizations in theology tend to eclipse difference and otherness; and wherever difference and otherness are eclipsed, that which is defined as "outside the norm" is usually debased and regarded as either less important, irrelevant, or even deviant. A good example is that women's spiritual experiences and writings have been bracketed out of the Christian record to a large degree.

10. Brock and Parker, *Proverbs of Ashes*, 20–22.

11. Ellen T. Charry, *By the Renewing of Your Minds: The Pastoral Function of Christian Doctrine* (New York: Oxford University Press, 1997), 182.

12. For one of the earliest and now-classic expressions of this critique, see Joanne Carlson Brown and Rebecca Parker, "For God So Loved the World?" in *Christianity, Patriarchy, and Abuse: A Feminist Critique,* ed. Joanne Carlson Brown and Carole R. Bohn (New York: Pilgrim Press, 1989), 1–30. Carter Heyward builds on this same trajectory of critique, but further argues that traditional atonement theology has other deleterious effects. Any theory that makes Jesus' suffering necessary and redemptive, argues Heyward, undercuts the value of human suffering by making Jesus' suffering appear unique. Traditional theories also lend an aura of the sacred to power that asserts itself by domination, argues Heyward. See Heyward, *Saving Jesus from Those Who Are Right: Rethinking What It Means to Be Christian* (Minneapolis: Fortress, 1999).

13. Delores Williams, *Sisters in the Wilderness: The Challenge of Womanist God-Talk* (Maryknoll: Orbis, 1993), 162.

14. This approach to the reconstruction of redemption undergirds the work of Carter Heyward, *Saving Jesus*; Rita Nakashima Brock, *Journeys by Heart: A Christology of Erotic Power* (New York: Crossroad, 1988); and Parker and Brown, *Proverbs of Ashes*.

15. Charry, *By the Renewing of Your Minds*, 4–10.

16. Ibid., 18–19.

17. John Cavadini, "'The Tree of Silly Fruit:' Images of the Cross in St. Augustine," in *The Cross in Christian Tradition from Paul to Bonaventure,* ed. Elizabeth A. Dreyer (New York: Paulist Press, 2000), 147.

18. Charry, *By the Renewing*, 10.

19. Ibid., 6–7.

20. Edward Farley, *Theologia: The Fragmentation and Unity of Theological Education* (Philadelphia: Fortress, 1983), 33–44.

21. Notably, when Schmiechen illustrates each of the ten theories he discusses in his comprehensive survey of atonement types, he appeals to the history of Christian doctrine. In no case does the material that he chooses to illustrate one of the theories take sermonic form. Instead, these theories are developed within debates concerning the "grammar" of atonement among theologians in church and academy. Schmiechen, *Saving Power*, 271–87.

22. See Hall, *Cross in Our Context*, 16–24. An engaging treatment of the emergence of Luther's theology of the cross in its historical context can be found in Deanna A. Thompson, *Crossing the Divide: Luther, Feminism, and the Cross* (Minneapolis: Augsburg Press, 2004), 15–28. Also in the contemporary "theology of the cross" tradition is Alister McGrath, *The Enigma of the Cross* (London: Hodder & Stoughton, 1987).

23. Martin Luther, *Luther's Works*, 31:41.

24. Charles Cousar cites Jürgen Moltmann and Eberhard Jüngel as major proponents of Luther's theology of the cross in Germany, and Douglas John Hall as its major spokesperson in the North American context. The concept of a "thin tradition" constituted by the pursuit of theology of the cross is from Douglas John Hall, *Lighten Our Darkness: Toward an Indigenous Theology of the Cross,* rev. ed. (Lima, OH: Academic Renewal Press, 2001), 117–35, as Cousar notes. See Charles B. Cousar, *A Theology of the Cross: The Death of Jesus in the Pauline Letters* (Minneapolis: Fortress Press, 1990), 8. Some contemporary theological proposals that extend this "thin tradition," in addition to those that Hall discusses, include Alan E. Lewis, *Between Cross and Resurrection: A Theology of Holy Saturday* (Grand Rapids: Eerdmans, 2001); Mary M. Solberg, *Compelling Knowledge: A Feminist Proposal for an Epistemology of the Cross* (Albany: State University of New York Press, 1997); Alberto L. García and A. R. Victor Raj, *Theology of the Cross for the Twenty-first Century*; and Deanna A. Thompson, *Crossing the Divide.*

25. Thompson, *Crossing the Divide*, 23.

26. Ibid., 22–23.

27. Hall, *Lighten Our Darkness*, 93–98.

28. Van Biema, "Why Did Jesus Die?" 57.

29. Hall, *Cross in Our Context*, 33.

30. Ibid., 32–33.

31. Hall, *Lighten Our Darkness*, 104.

32. Thompson, *Crossing the Divide*, 97–138.

33. Leonardo Boff, *Passion of Christ, Passion of the World* (Maryknoll, NY: Orbis Books, 1987), 83.

34. Alberto L. García, "Signposts for Global Witness," in García and Raj, *Theology of the Cross for the Twenty-first Century*, 27, 31.

35. John Nunes, "The African American Experience and Theology of the Cross," in García and Raj, *Theology of the Cross for the Twenty-first Century*, 230.

36. Leonora Tubbs Tisdale, *Preaching as Local Theology and Folk Art* (Minneapolis: Fortres Press, 1997), 110–21.

2. From Theory to Metaphor

1. See, for example, Gerhard Ebeling, "Word of God and Hermeneutic," in *The New Hermeneutic*, ed. James M. Robinson and John B. Cobb Jr. (New York: Harper & Row, 1964), 78–110. In a characteristic statement, Ebeling asserts, "Word is, strictly speaking, happening word. It is not enough to inquire into its intrinsic meaning, but that must be joined up with the question of its future, of what it effects" (103). The implication is that biblical texts are events of meaning that, through preaching, take place in the presence of contemporary listeners.

2. See Thomas G. Long, *The Witness of Preaching*, 2nd ed. (Louisville: Westminster John Knox Press, 2004), 11–51, 99–116.

3. Gail R. O'Day, "Toward a Biblical Theology of Preaching," in *Listening to the Word: Studies in Honor of Fred B. Craddock*, ed. Thomas G. Long and Gail R. O'Day (Nashville: Abingdon Press, 1993), 19, with emphasis added.

4. Kelsey, *Imagining Redemption*, 10.

5. Ibid, 15.

6. Cousar, *Theology of the Cross*, 2.

7. Victor Paul Furnish, "Theology and Ministry in the Pauline Letters," in *A Biblical Basis for Ministry*, ed. Earl E. Shelp and Ronald Sunderland (Philadelphia: Westminster Press, 1981), 101, 102.

8. J. Christiaan Beker, *The Triumph of God: The Essence of Paul's Thought* (Minneapolis: Fortress Press, 1990), ix–xvi. Beker discusses Paul's apocalyptic theological worldview as the organizing center of coherence of his theology, which nevertheless exhibits pastoral adaptability; see xi–xvi, 61–103, and 113–16.

9. Ibid., x–xi.

10. John Driver has also emphasized that New Testament writers worked with images of atonement, not theories, connecting them with human experience. See Driver, *Understanding the Atonement for the Mission of the Church* (Scottsdale, PA: Herald Press, 1986), 15–19.

11. Colin Gunton, *The Actuality of Atonement: A Study of Metaphor, Rationality, and the Christian Tradition*, Continuum reprint (London: T&T Clark, 2003), 1–32.

12. Ibid., 30.

13. Aristotle, *Poetics*, in *The Basic Works of Aristotle,* ed. Richard McKeon (New York: Random House, 1941), 1457b.6–9.

14. I. A. Richards, *The Philosophy of Rhetoric*, 2nd ed. (Oxford: Oxford University Press, 1971), 96; cited by Paul Ricoeur, *The Rule of Metaphor: Multi-disciplinary Studies of the Creation of Meaning in Language,* trans. Robert Czerny with Kathleen McLaughlin and John Costello (Toronto: University of Toronto Press,1977), 80.

15. Ricoeur, *Rule of Metaphor,* 152–53.

16. Ibid., 98.

17. Ibid., 246–47.

18. Thelma Megill-Cobbler, "Women and the Cross: Atonement in Rosemary Radford Ruether and Dorothee Soelle" (diss., Princeton Theological Seminary, 1992), 114.

19. The term "semantic impertinence" is borrowed from Paul Ricoeur, who in turn derives it from the work of Max Black. See Ricoeur, *Rule of Metaphor*, 152–53.

20. Colin Gunton, *Actuality of Atonement*, 44–52, 77–82.

21. On metaphors and models in scientific inquiry, Gunton (*Actuality of Atonement,* 31) cites the work of Richard Boyd, "Metaphor and Theory Change: What Is 'Metaphor' a Metaphor For?" in *Metaphor and Thought,* ed. A. Ortony (Cambridge: Cambridge University Press, 1979), 356–408.

22. For an especially rich discussion of the sacrifice motif in atonement language, emphasizing that the sacrifice of the cross is *God's* own offering of God's self in Jesus, see John Moses, *The Sacrifice of God: A Holistic Theory of Atonement* (Norwich: Canterbury Press, 1992).

23. J. Wentzel van Huyssteen, *Theology and the Justification of Faith: Constructing Theories in Systematic Theology* (Grand Rapids: Eerdmans, 1989), 135.

24. Ibid., 137. Van Huyssteen elaborates: "Language does not merely represent or reflect reality; it also *constitutes* reality. In this sense, language opens up, both creatively and exploratively the reality of which we speak, since what we see as reality is to a large extent creatively and exploratively *determined* by the metaphoric potential of the language in which reality is articulated" (ibid., 137–38). Van Huyssteen's constructivist, critical-realist approach contrasts with that of Gunton, who construes metaphors of atonement as disclosive keys that grant us access to the "ontology" of divine-human relationality (*Actuality of Atonement*, 45–46). For further discussion of critical realism, see van Huyssteen, *Theology and the Justification of Faith*, 143–97; and Niels Henrik Gregersen and J. Wentzel van Huyssteen, eds., *Rethinking Theology and Science: Six Models for the Current Dialogue* (Grand Rapids: Eerdmans, 1998), 51–86.

25. Sallie McFague, *Models of God: Theology for an Ecological, Nuclear Age* (Philadelphia: Fortress Press, 1987), 35.

26. McFague, *Metaphorical Theology: Models of God in Religious Language* (Philadelphia: Fortress Press, 1982), 145–92.

27. Ibid., 23.

28. Ibid., 24.

29. Cousar, *Theology of the Cross*, 85.

30. Ibid., 87.

31. Gunton, *Actuality of Atonement*, 34.

32. Cousar, *Theology of the Cross*, 20.

33. An example of a metaphor of redemption that is only lightly treated in the canon but figures prominently in the early centuries of the church is the deliverance of captives from the clutches of Satan. This metaphor is favored by many of the church fathers, notably Irenaeus, Gregory of Nyssa, and Athanasius. See Schmiechen, *Saving Power*, 125–30.

34. Renita J. Weems, *Battered Love: Marriage, Sex, and Violence in the Hebrew Prophets* (Minneapolis: Fortress Press, 1995), 7.

35. Schmiechen, *Sharing Power*, 313–27.

36. Kelsey, *Imagining Redemption*, 41.

37. George Lindbeck, *The Nature of Doctrine* (Philadelphia: Westminster Press, 1984), 81.

38. Schmiechen, *Saving Power*, 5.

39. Ibid., 5.

40. Kelsey, *Imagining Redemption*, 15.

3. Challenging Cross Talk Gone Wrong

1. See Segovia and Tolbert, *Reading from This Place,* 2 vols.

2. Joanne Carlson Brown and Rebecca Parker, "For God So Loved the World?" in Brown and Bohn, *Christianity, Patriarchy, and Abuse*, 9. See also Joanne Carlson Brown, "Divine Child Abuse?" *Daughters of Sarah,* Summer 1992, 24.

3. Leanne Van Dyk, "Do Theories of Atonement Foster Abuse?" *Dialog* 35 (Winter 1996): 24.

4. Ray, *Deceiving the Devil,* 25. Ray devotes half of the first chapter of the book to the feminist and womanist critique of traditional, patriarchal definitions of sin. As she notes, the groundbreaking article on the subject of sin reconsidered in a feminist perspective was by Valerie Saiving, "The Human Situation: A Feminine View," in *Womanspirit Rising: A Feminist Reader in Religion,* ed. Carol Christ and Judith Plaskow (San Francisco: Harper & Row, 1979), 25–42.

5. Hall, *Cross in Our Context*, 93.

6. James Cone, *God of the Oppressed* (London: SPCK, 1977), 211–12.

7. Cited by Alberto L. García, "The Witness of the Cross in Light of the Hispanic Experience," in García and Raj, *Theology of the Cross,* 189–90.

8. Ray, *Deceiving the Devil*, 89, emphasis hers. Ray helpfully summarizes postcolonialist atonement critiques and the way these approaches can resource fresh

thinking about the Christian doctrine of atonement in chap. 4, "Cross and Sword," and chap. 5, "Atonement from the Underside," 71–101.

9. L. Susan Bond, *Trouble with Jesus*, 74.

10. Hall, *Cross in Our Context*, 107.

11. Gorringe, *God's Just Vengeance*, 224.

12. Ibid., 12.

13. Ibid., 7.

14. Weaver, *Nonviolent Atonement*, 225.

15. Ibid., 71.

16. Ibid., 19.

17. Ray, *Deceiving the Devil*, 55 (emphasis hers).

18. In addition to the work of Weaver and Gorringe, see Bartlett, *Cross Purposes*.

19. Green and Baker, *Recovering the Scandal of the Cross*, 140.

20. Ray, *Deceiving the Devil*, 2.

21. Michael Northcutt, "The Gospel of the Cross Confronts the Powers," in Barrow and Bartley, *Consuming Passion*, 95.

22. John Calvin, *Institutes of the Christian Religion* 2.16.2–3, trans. Henry Beveridge (Grand Rapids: Eerdmans, 1975), 1:435.

23. The insight that Christ was a knowing and willing volunteer for the suffering of the cross is cited by William C. Placher, *Jesus the Savior: The Meaning of Jesus Christ for Christian Faith* (Louisville: Westminster John Knox Press, 2001), 139. For Placher, this insight alone by no means resolves the problems with single-theory or overly literalized versions of atonement theory; it is mentioned in the context of a discerning discussion of the problems of portraying God in atonement as an enraged father.

24. Green and Baker, *Recovering the Scandal of the Cross*, 146–50.

25. Steve Chalke, "Redeeming the Cross from Death to Life," in Barrow and Bartley, *Consuming Passion*, 21.

26. Green and Baker, *Recovering the Scandal of the Cross*, 142–150.

27. Schmiechen, *Saving Power*, 113.

28. Paul Fiddes, *Past Event and Present Salvation: The Christian Idea of Atonement* (Louisville: Westminster John Knox Press, 1989), 99.

29. Ibid., 105.

30. Boersma, *Violence, Hospitality, and the Cross*, 105.

31. Ibid., 164.

32. Kathryn Tanner, *Jesus, Humanity, and the Trinity: A Brief Systematic Theology* (Minneapolis: Fortress, 2001), 67–95.

33. Boersma, *Violence, Hospitality, and the Cross*, 177.

34. This phrase comes from a sermon by Frank Strasburger delivered at Trinity Episcopal Church, Princeton, NJ, June 17, 2007.

35. Ray, *Deceiving the Devil*, 69.

36. Ibid, 71.

37. Terrell, *Power in the Blood?* 121–25.

38. Ibid., 116. These remarks occur in the context of Ray's discussion of a necessarily "tragic" view of knowledge and experience in which complexity and ambiguity are unavoidable and need to be honored, methodologically. See chap. 6, "Mending and Discarding," 102–17.

39. Ray, *Deceiving the Devil*, 103.

40. Ibid., 116.

41. For a discussion of the way that assumptions about culture, theology, and the use of Scripture are already "coded" into any given preaching context before one begins to preach, see John S. McClure, *The Four Codes of Preaching: Rhetorical Strategies* (Minneapolis: Fortress Press, 1991).

42. See Tisdale, "Exegeting the Congregation," in *Preaching as Local Theology and Folk Art*, 56–90.

43. Paul W. Kummer, "Held in His Arms," in *From This Day Forward: First Lesson Sermons for Lent/Easter, Cycle B* (Lima, OH: CSS Publishing, 1999), 47–52.

44. Ibid., 49.

45. Ibid.

46. Barbara Brown Taylor, "The Will of God," in *God in Pain: Teaching Sermons about Suffering* (Nashville: Abingdon Press, 1998), 116.

47. Ibid., 118.

48. Ibid.

49. Laurie J. Ferguson, "Jesus Not a Victim for Our Sins," in *The Book of Women's Sermons: Hearing God in Each Other's Voices*, ed. E. Lee Hancock (New York: Riverhead Books, 1999), 100–104.

50. Ibid., 100.

51. Ibid., 101.

52. Ibid.

53. Ibid.

54. Ibid., 102.

55. Ibid., 102–3.

56. Ibid.

57. Ibid., 103–4.

58. Marilyn McCord Adams, "Crucified God: Abuser or Redeemer?" in *Wrestling for Blessing* (New York: Church Publishing Inc., 2005), 49–54.

59. Ibid., 51.

60. Ibid.; italics hers.

61. Ibid., 52.

62. Ibid.

63. Ibid.

64. Ibid., 53–54.

65. Ibid., 54.

4. God in Pain

1. Nancy J. Duff, "Atonement and the Christian Life," 31.

2. Barbara Reid, "The Cross and Cycles of Violence," *Interpretation* 58, no. 4 (October 2004): 378.

3. Ibid., 383.

4. Ibid., 380.

5. Ibid., 384.

6. J. Christiaan Beker, *Suffering and Hope: The Biblical Vision and the Human Predicament*, 2nd ed. (Grand Rapids: Eerdmans, 1994), 25–26.

7. Ibid., 26.

8. Marilyn McCord Adams, *Horrendous Evils and the Goodness of God* (Ithaca, NY: Cornell University Press, 1999), 28.

9. Kelsey, *Imagining Redemption*, 47.

10. Ibid., 79.

11. Ibid., 82.

12. Martyn develops this view succinctly in "The Apocalyptic Gospel in Galatians," *Interpretation* 54, no. 1 (July 2000): 246–66. The phrase "turning of the ages" occurs in the writing of Rudolf Bultmann; in speaking of the dawning of the reign of God, he writes, "Paul looks back; *the turning point of the ages has already come (die Wende der Äonen ist schon erfolgt).*" Bultmann, *Glauben und Verstehen,* vol. 2. (Tübingen: J. C. B. Mohr, 1958), 200; emphasis his. Martyn takes up the phrase "turning of the ages" in many of his writings on Paul's interpretation of the cross, arguing that only when we take into account that Paul sees the cross as the "turning point of the ages" can we understand the rhetoric of key passages, particularly in 1 and 2 Corinthians, Romans, and Galatians. See also "Epistemology at the Turn of the Ages," in *Theological Issues in the Letters of Paul* (Nashville: Abingdon, 1997), 92–95, 109–10; "From Paul to Flannery O'Connor with the Power of Grace," in *Theological Issues*, 285; and Martyn's Galatians commentary, *Galatians: A New Translation with Introduction and Commentary,* Anchor Bible (New York: Doubleday, 1997), 22–23, 95–105.

13. Martyn, "From Paul to Flannery O'Connor," 285.

14. Homiletical theologian James F. Kay makes a compelling argument as well, that a fundamentally apocalyptic conception of the cross's significance and ontological effect is key to understanding Paul's new-creation cosmology and epistemology. This in turn, Kay argues, governs Paul's understanding of what preaching is and what it effects. In this apocalyptic perspective, the preaching of the cross itself *effects* the apocalyptic "turning of the ages." Preaching "according to the cross" places in crisis worldly epistemology, power, and rhetoric. See Kay, "The Word of the Cross at the Turn of the Ages," *Interpretation* 53, no. 1 (January 1999): 44–56, esp. 44–48.

15. Bartlett, *Cross Purposes*, 18.

16. Ibid., 138.

17. The concept of the "defeat" of horrors is developed by Marilyn McCord

Adams in chap. 5, "Resources to the Rescue," in *Horrendous Evils and the Goodness of God*, 155–80.

18. See, for example, the arguments for and against the redemptive potential of the cross for black women in JoAnne Marie Terrell, *Power in the Blood?* and in Delores Williams, *Sisters in the Wilderness*. The essence of their arguments can also be accessed in two recently published essays: see Williams, "Black Women's Surrogacy Experience and the Christian Notion of Redemption," and Terrell, "Our Mother's Gardens: Rethinking Sacrifice," both in *Cross Examinations: Readings on the Meaning of the Cross Today*, ed. Marit Trelstad (Minneapolis: Augsburg Fortress, 2006), 19–49.

19. Blount, *Can I Get a Witness?* 73.

20. Ibid., 73.

21. A version of this lecture was delivered, as well, as the Ingersoll Lecture, October 19, 2006, at Harvard University Divinity School, and may be heard online at http://www.hds.harvard.edu/news/events_online/ingersoll_2006.html.

22. J. Alfred Smith Sr., "An American Scandal: The Crisis of the Crucified," *The African American Pulpit* 1, no. 3 (Summer 1998): 63–64.

23. Ibid., 63.

24. Ibid., 65–66.

25. Morris Harrison Tynes, "The Greatest Proof," in *Outstanding Black Sermons*, vol. 2 (Valley Forge, PA: Judson Press, 1979), 125.

26. Kenneth Leech, "Healed by His Wounds," in *We Preach Christ Crucified: The Proclamation of the Cross in a Dark Age* (Boston: Cowley Publications, 1994), 20–38.

27. Ibid., 23.

28. Ibid., 23–24.

29. Ibid., 26–28.

30. Ibid., 29.

31. Ibid., 30.

32. Barbara Brown Taylor, "The Silence of God," in *God in Pain*, 111.

33. Ibid., 112–13.

34. Stanley Hauerwas, "The Sixth Word," in *Cross-Shattered Christ: Meditations on the Seven Last Words* (Grand Rapids: Brazos Press, 2004), 83–90.

35. Ibid., 85.

36. Ibid.

37. Ibid., 86.

38. Ibid., 90.

5. God's Weakness

1. Theologians such as John Howard Yoder, Stanley Hauerwas, and J. Denny Weaver develop this view.

2. Schmiechen (*Saving Power*, 195–96) expresses concern about misrepresentations of Anselm by L. Susan Bond (*Trouble with Jesus*) and J. Denny Weaver

(*Nonviolent Atonement*), both of whom read Anselm's satisfaction model in close association with penal substitution theory, with the result that they not only lay at Anselm's doorstep responsibility for the failures of the latter paradigm, but also fail to see any positive potential in the satisfaction view.

3. Schmiechen, *Saving Power*, 202–3.

4. Ibid., 213.

5. Ibid., 271–87.

6. Ibid., 272.

7. Ibid., 277, with his parentheses.

8. Ibid.

9. Paula M. Cooey, "The Redemption of the Body: Post-Patriarchal Reconstruction of Inherited Christian Doctrine," in *After Patriarchy: Feminist Transformations of the World Religions*, ed. Paula M. Cooey, William R. Eakin, and Jay B. McDaniel (Maryknoll, NY: Orbis Books, 1991), 120.

10. James C. Goodloe IV, "Christ Has Broken Down the Wall!" *Lectionary Homiletics* 8, no. 8 (July 1997): 22–24.

11. Ibid., 23.

12. Ibid.

13. Ibid.

14. Adams, *Wrestling for a Blessing*, 57–58.

15. Ibid.

16. Ibid., 60.

17. For a full presentation of this discussion, see Blount, *Can I Get a Witness?* chap. 3, "Wreaking Weakness: The Way of the Lamb."

18. Ibid., 70.

19. Ibid., 70–71.

20. Ibid., 70.

21. Ibid., 78.

22. Ibid., 87.

23. Ibid., 69.

24. The phrase is part of the title of Blount's chapter on the slaughtered-Lamb figure.

25. Stanley M. Hauerwas, "The Fourth Word," in *Cross-Shattered Christ: Meditations on the Seven Last Words* (Grand Rapids: Brazos Press, 2004), 59.

26. Ibid., 60.

27. Ibid., 62–63.

28. Ibid., 64.

29. Ibid., 65.

30. See René Girard, *Violence and the Sacred* (Baltimore: Johns Hopkins University Press, 1977).

31. S. Mark Heim, *Saved from Sacrifice*. For another, more-philosophically driven approach to the subject, see Bartlett, *Cross Purposes*.

32. Heim, *Saved from Sacrifice*, 64.

33. Ibid., 91.

34. Ibid., 114.

35. Ibid., 131–33.

36. Ibid., 146–47.

37. Barbara Brown Taylor, "The Myth of Redemptive Violence," in *God in Pain,* 106–9.

38. Ibid., 108.

39. Ibid., 109.

40. Ibid.

41. Debbie Blue, "A Different Story," in *Proclaiming the Scandal of the Cross: Contemporary Images of Atonement,* ed. Mark D. Baker (Grand Rapids: Baker Academic, 2006), 62.

42. Ibid., 67.

43. Ibid., 68.

44. Ibid.

45. At the sermon's close, Blue retreats a step from her claim that the undermining of the scapegoat mechanism at the cross is decisive and objective. She reintroduces the idea that we have a choice to make *between* two alternative stories, the story of scapegoating violence (which, Blue admits, seems in a limited way to "work" to stabilize relations between warring parties) or "this utterly different, life-giving story," which "frees us for communion based . . . on the transforming, forgiving love of God" (ibid., 70).

46. See, for example, Boersma, *Violence, Hospitality, and the Cross*; Kenneth R. Chase and Alan Jacobs, *Must Christianity Be Violent? Reflections on History, Practice, and Theology* (Grand Rapids: Brazos Press, 2003); and Weaver, *Nonviolent Atonement.*

6. Jesus' Death as Sacrifice

1. Fiddes, *Past Event and Present Salvation*, 61. See also S. W. Sykes, "Introduction," in *Sacrifice and Redemption,* ed. S. W. Sykes (Cambridge: Cambridge University Press, 1991), 18.

2. John Moses, *The Sacrifice of God,* 122.

3. *The Book of Common Prayer* (New York: Seabury Press, 1978), 362.

4. Williams, "Black Women's Surrogacy Experience and the Christian Notion of Redemption," in Trelstad, *Cross Examinations*, 32.

5. Terrell, *Power in the Blood?* 124–25.

6. Fiddes, *Past Event and Present Salvation*, 61. The term "slippage" is Fiddes's.

7. William Cowper, "There Is a Fountain Filled with Blood," *The Hymnbook* (New York: Presbyterian Church in the U.S., United Presbyterian Church in the U.S.A., and Reformed Church in America, 1955), 239.

8. Schmiechen, *Saving Power,* 22.

9. Weaver, *Nonviolent Atonement,* 59.

10. For a discussion of the semantic range of sacrificial understanding in Jewish and Hellenistic contexts, see Fiddes, *Past Event and Present Salvation*, 61–75. Frances Young provides a brief overview of the meaning and function of sacrifice in the religions of the ancient world and particularly in the Jewish cult in *Sacrifice and the Death of Christ* (London: SPCK, 1975), 21–46. See also D. R. Jones, "Sacrifice and Holiness," in Sykes, *Sacrifice and Redemption*, 9–21; and John Moses, *The Sacrifice of God*, 63–77.

11. Fiddes, *Past Event and Present Salvation*, 67.

12. Edward Hulmes, "The Semantics of Sacrifice," in Sykes, *Sacrifice and Redemption*, 265.

13. J. D. G. Dunn, "Paul's Understanding of the Death of Jesus as Sacrifice," in Sykes, *Sacrifice and Redemption*, 35–56; Gunton, *Actuality of Atonement*, 136.

14. Sallie McFague, *Models of God*, 37, 41, 43; Bond, *Trouble with Jesus*, 28.

15. The rhetorical functions of correction, challenge, and displacement are closely related to three of the homiletical strategies for transforming local congregational imagination discussed earlier, as described by Leonora Tubbs Tisdale in *Preaching as Local Theology and Folk Art*.

16. See Young, *Sacrifice and the Death of Christ*, 24–31. Other sources that explore the life-creating trajectory of sacrifice include Bartlett, *Cross Purposes*, 198–209; S. W. Sykes, "Sacrifice in the New Testament and Christian Theology," in *Sacrifice*, ed. M. F. C. Bertillon and Meyer Fortes (London: Academic Press, 1980), 61–83; Weaver, *Nonviolent Atonement*, 58–66; and David Wheeler, "The Cross and the Blood: Dead or Living Images?" *Dialog* 35, no. 1 (Winter 1996): 8–13.

17. Young, *Sacrifice and the Death of Christ*, 79.

18. Ian Bradley, *The Power of Sacrifice* (London: Darton, Longman & Todd, 1995), 9. Bradley's treatment of Jesus' death as sacrifice is only partly satisfying: he tries to establish that a pattern of life-death-life is inherent in the being of God and creation—which does not seem to illuminate the cross as atoning.

19. Gunton, *Actuality of Atonement*, 129–30.

20. Tanner, *Jesus, Humanity, and the Trinity*, 71.

21. Ibid., 75–76.

22. John Moses, *Sacrifice of God*, 159.

23. Fiddes, *Past Event and Present Salvation*, 82.

24. S. W. Sykes, "Outline of a Theology of Sacrifice," in Sykes, *Sacrifice and Redemption*, 286, 290.

25. A. N. Chester, "Hebrews: The Final Sacrifice," in Sykes, *Sacrifice and Redemption,* 57–72.

26. Mary J. Streufert, "Maternal Sacrifice as a Hermeneutics of the Cross," in Trelstad, *Cross Examinations*, 64.

27. Ibid., 75.

28. Tanner, *Jesus, Humanity, and the Trinity*, 88.

29. Toyohiko Kagawa, *Meditations on the Cross*, trans. Helen F. Topping and Marion R. Draper (Chicago: Willett, Clark, 1935).

30. Ibid., 97–98.

31. Ibid., 67.

32. Ibid., 206.

33. Ibid., 206–7.

34. Ibid., 207.

35. Ibid., 206–7. Kagawa's own relation to the labor movement in Japan was complex. Initially, he supported the labor movement and thought strikes were necessary, suffering imprisonment for his participation in widespread labor strikes in Kobe and Osaka in the summer of 1921. Later, however, Kagawa became convinced that the labor movement was being manipulated by communist influences, and therefore he opposed what he regarded as unnecessary, frequent strike actions. See his unnumbered note, on 208–9.

36. Ibid., 210.

37. Ibid., 110.

38. Ibid.

39. Fleming Rutledge, "A Cross at Ground Zero," in *Undoing of Death,* 228.

40. Ibid., 229.

41. Ibid., 231.

42. Ibid., 231.

43. Ibid., 232.

7. Open Gestures toward Mystery

1. Robert S. Paul, *The Atonement and the Sacraments: The Relation of the Atonement to the Sacraments of Baptism and the Lord's Supper* (Nashville: Abingdon, 1960), 307–8.

2. Ibid., 308–9.

3. Ibid., 369–70.

4. Ibid., 383.

5. I owe the arresting insight that Christ "places himself in our hands" at the table—hands himself over to us (Greek: *paradidomi*)—to Dr. Iain R. Torrance, President of Princeton Seminary; communion homily, Miller Chapel, Princeton Theological Seminary, April 21, 2006.

6. Calvin, *Institutes* 4.17.10–12 (Eerdmans), 2:562–65.

7. "Holy Eucharist: Rite One," *The Book of Common Prayer* (New York: Church Publishing Inc., 1979), 333–42.

8. "Holy Eucharist: Rite Two," *Book of Common Prayer,* 362.

9. Ibid., 368.

10. Ibid., 370.

11. "Service for the Lord's Day—Order with Texts," *Book of Common Worship* (Louisville: Westminster/John Knox Press, 1993), 70–71.

12. Ibid., 127, 131, 140, 143, 147.

13. Ibid., 150.

14. "Communion Prayer," #614 in *Chalice Worship* (St. Louis: Chalice Press, 1997), 410.

15. Ibid., 82.

16. *Book of Worship: United Church of Christ* (New York: United Church of Christ Office for Church Life and Leadership, 1986), 46. The reference to sacrifice in the invitation to the table occurs in Service of Word and Sacrament II, p. 66.

17. Ibid., 92.

18. *Book of Common Worship*, 410–11.

19. Ibid., 424.

20. Ibid., 427.

21. Here I am citing the revised text of this traditional hymn, which avoids hierarchical language as well as male pronouns for God. Original hymn text by Henry Francis Lyte, 1864; revision by Ecumenical Women's Council, 1974: "Praise, My Soul, the God of Heaven," #479 in *The Presbyterian Hymnal* (Louisville: Westminster/John Knox Press, 1990).

22. Hymn text by Philip F. Hiller, 1767; trans. by Esther Bergen, 1959; "All My Sins Have Been Forgiven," #291 in *Hymns for the Living Church* (Carol Stream, IL: Hope Publishing, 1974).

23. James Gertmenian, "Throughout These Lenten Days and Nights," #129 in *Sing! A New Creation* (Grand Rapids: CRC Publications, 2001).

24. Hymn text by Király Imre von Pécselyi, Hungarian; trans. Erik Routley; "There in God's Garden," #138 in *Sing! A New Creation*.

25. Information on the "emergent" church, including lists of relevant publications, can be found at http://emergingchurch.info/links/index.htm and www.emergentvillage.org.

26. A helpful resource is www.cyberhymnal.org. Both texts and tunes can be sought by theme, keyword, or season.

27. Angela M. Edwards, "Sprinkle This Blood," *African-American Pulpit* 4, no. 3 (Summer 2001): 45–49. Edwards's sermon may be compared to that of Frank Thomas, "Sprinkle This Blood," *African-American Pulpit* 2, no. 4 (Fall 1999): 68–72.

28. Edwards, "Sprinkle This Blood," 46.

29. Ibid., 47.

30. Ibid., 48.

31. Barbara Brown Taylor, "Blood Covenant," in *Gospel Medicine* (Boston: Cowley Publications, 1995), 58–59.

32. Ibid., 61.

33. Ibid., 62.

34. Ibid., 63.

35. Ibid.

36. Boersma, *Violence, Hospitality, and the Cross*, 109–11. In this discussion, Boersma follows closely the work of Vincent Brümmer, *The Model of Love: A Study in Philosophical Theology* (Cambridge: Cambridge University Press, 1993).

37. Bond, *Trouble with Jesus*, 133.

38. Ibid., 110–11. Bond constructs her criteria with a view to the work of M. Thomas Thangaraj, who himself commends similar criteria to be applied in the

quest for theologically adequate, contextual Christologies. See M. Thomas
Thangaraj. *The Crucified Guru: An Experiment in Cross-Cultural Christology*
(Nashville: Abingdon, 1994).

39. Ibid., 110–11.
40. Ibid., 128.
41. Ibid., 121.
42. Ibid., 125.
43. Ibid., 142.
44. Ibid., 129.
45. Van Dyk, "Do Theories of Atonement Foster Abuse?" 25.

Index